IMAGINATION MOTEL

CHUCK KINDER

SIX GALLERY PRESS

IMAGINATION MOTEL © 2014 by Chuck Kinder
ISBN: 978-1-926616-65-0
Cover by Beth Steidle
Published by Six Gallery Press
First Printing: Fall 2014

IMAGINATION MOTEL

STARRING RAINY MCCALL AS THE OLD SORCERER'S DAUGHTER, WANTON HIPPIE PRINCESS FROM THE LOST AGE OF AQUARIUS …

A TOME OF POMES THAT, LIKE SUBATOMIC PARTICLES, CAN APPEAR IN TWO DIFFERENT PLACES AT ONCE, MOVE FORWARD AND BACKWARD IN TIME, BEHAVING LIKE BOTH A PARTICLE AND A WAVE OF LIGHT AND MEANING …

A TOME WHICH OPENS IN A SHABBY OFFICE WHERE AN OLD MOTEL MANAGER AND SOMETIME SORCERER FEEDS A HALF DOZEN OR SO ANGEL FISH GLIDING IN A SMALL AQUARIUM LIKE THE GHOSTLY MEMORIES OF TINY MERMAIDS BENEATH THE WAVES OF AN ANCIENT FORGOTTEN SEA, FISH THAT THE WANTON HIPPIE PRINCESS RAINY MCCALL NAMES LIKE NEW PETS …

IMAGINATION MOTEL BLINKS THE SPUTTERING BLUE NEON SIGN IN THE OFFICE WINDOW OF THE PASTEL PINK, LOW-SLUNG STUCCO BUILDING ON A SIDE STREET OF CLOSED SALOONS, SHADOWS, AND SECRETS AT THE OLD JAGGED EDGE OF TOWN NEAR THE SHORE, THE PARKING LOT PACKED WITH CARS LIKE A DRIVE-IN MOVIE, INCOGNITO AND INCONSOLABLE AS GIANT SEA TURTLES DREAMING IN THE MOONLIGHT OF LOST ISLAND KINGDOMS OF ILLUSION …

POMES WITH MANY BAGS OF BUTTERED POPCORN AND BIG PEPSIS

BY CHUCK KINDER

Everything I write is pure thanks to my wife & gunmoll & copoet
for pushing forty years, Diane Cecily
& to my mother Eileen, who read to me daily from
Robert Louis Stevenson's A Child's Garden of Verses
until I ran away from home at age seventeen in order to become a bandit
& famous beatnik poet

PROGRAM:
THE COMPLETE POEMOGRAPHY

A
TARZAN AND HIS MATE

B
HIGH SIERRA

C
STAGECOACH

D
THE MOLLY MAGUIRES

1. SOMETIMES POETS ARRIVE IN TOWN ON TRAINS FROM PITTSBURGH LATE AT NIGHT INCOGNITO, Poem with Soundtrack by Henry Mancini, Employing Irish Modal Harmony Played by Period Instruments Including the Irish Harp, Penny Whistle, and Squeezebox (28)
2. POETS NEVER GET ENOUGH, Poem Featuring Capital Punishment (30)

E
INVASION OF THE BODY SNATCHERS

1. THE NARROW ESCAPE OF CHILDHOOD SWEETHEARTS, Poem with Puppy, Old Cave Creatures Long Extinct, and Dreaming Bats (33)
2. THE LAST CHANCE TO DIE FOR LOVE, Poem with Magic Ring, Mushroom Race, Cave Bear Skull, Cold Lips, Mask of Invisibility, and Dripping Afterbirth (34)
3. THE LAST EGG OF LOVE (36)

F
THE ROMANCES OF RAINY MCCALL: TRAGIC WANTON HIPPIE PRINCESS FROM THE LOST AGE OF AQUARIUS OR THE OLD SORCERER'S DAUGHTER

1. GHOST HOLO-SIGNALS FROM THE TRAGIC DECADES OF BLACK AND WHITE TELEVISION, Poem with Christmas Lights, Trade Winds, and Hooker (39)
2. UNDERCOVER ASTRONAUT MAN: THE SECRET AGENDA OF THE AMERICAN SPACE PROGRAM, Installation Poem with Bikini Panties, Plump Planets, and Golf on the Moon (41)
3. MIDNIGHT MOVIES, Poem as Still Life with Radio and Oldies but Goodies by Elvis and Bobby Vinton (43)
4. ESCAPE VELOCITY, Poem with Patio, Starship, and Tall Frosty Highball, in Which Undercover Astronaut Man Is on the Verge of Getting Laid (45)
5. THE SOFT BLUE SUEDE GRAVITY OF LOVE, Poem with Fold-Out Bed and Body Parts (47)
6. GIANT NIGHT, The Paranormal Poetry of Chaos Theory with Cameo by Steve McQueen and Soundtrack Featuring Roy Orbison (48)
7. EVEN THE STARS MUST SOMETIMES GET LONELY, Poem with Pine Trees, Shotgun Blast, and Belt Buckle (49)
8. SKULL MOVIES, Poem with Dead Buffalo and Feathered Horns in a Dream Canyon Cinema (51)

IMAGINATION MOTEL

IMAGINATION MOTEL,
OR THE SECRET MEANING OF MOVIES, MOSTLY OLD AND IN BLACK AND
WHITE AS WATCHED ON SNOWY, LATE NIGHT TELEVISION IN CHEAP
MOTEL ROOMS OF LONGING, DESIRE, AND FLIGHT, LIGHT FLICKERING
ACROSS SPARKLING CEILINGS LIKE NIGHT SKIES THICK WITH GALAXIES
OR THE REFLECTION OF CAMPFIRES IN ANCIENT INDIAN DREAMING
CAVES ...

A
TARZAN AND HIS MATE

TARZAN AND HIS MATE (1934) is considered by most Tarzan fans to be the best of the Johnny Weissmuller-Maureen O'Sullivan Tarzan films. Surely it was the sexiest, with Weissmuller and especially O'Sullivan nearly naked during the film's 105-minute running time. Picking up where 1932's Tarzan the Ape Man left off, avaricious ivory hunters arrive in the African jungle in search of the fabled Elephants' Graveyard. Tarzan is shot and left for dead, but, rescued by his simian friends, Tarzan races toward the elephants' burial ground and its precious ivory, where the evil poachers have already been eaten by lions and Jane is next on their menu. But a convenient elephant stampede, heralded by that classic Tarzan yell: ahh-ee-yachhh-ee-yahhh, saves Jane from the lions' fangs in the nick of time.

Themes: treasure hunts, daring rescues
Tone: rousing, sweeping, tense
Keywords: civilization, elephant graveyard, hunting, ivory, jungle, lion, poacher

BACK IN HIGH SCHOOL WHEN JANE PLAYED TUBA
(Poem with Beautiful Quarterback and Blowjob)

In the marching band & Jane was brilliant
In Latin & editor of the yearbook
Jane was famous for giving exquisitely sensitive
Albeit dramatic head
But during Jane's extravagant going down
While Jane was merely disguised
As some beautiful quarterback's
Lap of bouncy hair
Jane would star
In passionate moviedreams of love
Rescue & escape
From Jane's sad, boring, brown-eyed
Failed, mousey, blowjob life
With happy endings
In Jane's passionate moviedreams
Jane is no longer a fatty & drab
& Jane's face is no longer
A pimple plantation
No, folks, Jane's flawless flesh
Is peaches & cream
Jane's tropical sun-kissed skin is golden as yellow roses & ripe
Jane's mane of hair blonde & luxuriant
& Jane's blue, eager eyes
Seem almost too large, too luminous
For Jane's fresh pretty petal of a face
This beautiful, blonde girl, Jane
(Probably a Lost Princess)
Discovers herself time after time
In great peril, & Jane is such
A delicate, helpless, albeit voluptuous
Little thing

Once, the creepy Clay-People discover a sad & sullen Jane
Lost & alone in the Sunken Forest
& since Tarzan is not on hand
To save Jane, Jane is easy
To capture. As Jane struggles & struggles
To twist free
From the crumbly fingers
Of the creepy Clay-People
The long sleek muscles
Of Jane's smooth arms & legs
Flex like the shadows of leaves & flowers
On flowing water
Much as the long hair of Jane's mother
Tangled in the twisted roots
Of Jane's father's tree

TARZAN IS HURRYING TO JANE NOW, NOW!
(Poem With Helpless Blonde Girl, Submerged Cave Creature, And Black Tragic Water)

As Jane struggles & struggles
To twist free from the crumbly clutch of the creepy Clay-People
Jane's Jungle Princess gown of spotted skins
Negligible to begin with
Is torn in revealing places, & now
A large section of Jane's smooth, downy tummy
Jane's supple left shoulder
& the soft upper swelling
Of Jane's perfect left melon of a blonde breast are bare
Deep in their hidden caves
The creepy Clay-People chain Jane
To a spongy pillar
Where the damp soil
Begins to hungrily engulf Jane
Like the movement of some madly sporing mold
Over moist, sweet white bread, or a waterfall of wildly flowing foam full of blind fish
The ravenous
Mud will spread over Jane's lovely flesh
Flesh like yellow roses luminous in moonlight
Until Jane too will become a zombie of goo
Deaf & dumb
A mud babe
Ugly as a turd
But this will never happen to Jane
Beautiful, sun-kissed, blonde girls are always rescued
In the nick of time
Tarzan is hurrying to Jane now, now!
Tarzan's hard muscled body arches
As Tarzan dives from the high cliffs
Ahh-ee-yachhh-ee-yahhh
Into the dangerous water far below
Dangerous deep dark water
A black lake with no bottom
(The local natives sing
In their creation songs)
Tarzan swims underwater, suspended
Seemingly in the fluid
Silvery center of Jane's moviedream
Dreaming itself to life
Floating between worlds
Waiting to be born
Tarzan rises like a bubble from the bottom
Of Jane's brain

Hooked & reeled by the light of Jane's moviedream of love
From his nightsea journey
To his real life's beginning in the waters
Of Jane's movie imagination
Tarzan swims into what is missing
With no shadow yet to trail behind him
Like a flickering fin
Tarzan does not see the starlight drifting on the surface
Of the dark water above him
Beneath Tarzan there are other water beings
& fish blind in the black water of midnight
Nobody has ever seen before
Beings & blind fish that
Like submerged stars blink
Deeper than thought or language
Like a wondrous water plant's blooming
Tarzan's hair sways & sweeps
About Tarzan's head
A halo of submerged light
Or the nearly luminescent wings of fish
Tarzan's bulging eyes are black with awareness
& expectation
Tarzan surfaces inside a cave
Whose moist shadowy ridged walls rise
High out of sight into unfathomable womblike darkness
Tarzan braces his arms upon a ledge that feels like wet flesh
Tarzan takes a well deserved breather
After a quick disembodied cry of relief: ahh-ee-yachhh-ee-yahhh
It happens in a heartbeat
The ropey muscles of Tarzan's shoulders shudder
Tarzan is pulled backwards into the tragic water
As waves of night rise about him
His skin seeing down deep beneath him, as it does in dark water
Tarzan chops desperately at the entangling tentacles
That pull Tarzan deeper & deeper
Into dark, tragic water murky as
Afterbirth

3

PUSSY-SIMPLE APEMAN
(Poem with Steaming Rainforests, Land Time Forgot, Perfume, and Ugly One-Eyed Angel)

The huge glowing eyes of the old creature are
Unblinking eyes, yellow, luminous
Wild with mourning
Tears flowing from them like falling stars
& yet there is no hatred
In those terrible eyes
& when Tarzan plunges at last
Knife in teeth toward them
There is no evident fear
& no evident pain
As Tarzan's knife slashes those tragic eyes open
Like the soft translucent flesh of testicles
& as milky foam spews
From those ragged wounds
Those torn, ancient eyes give no sign
Of terror or anger or anguish
Or even regret
Only a sort of sorrow maybe
That there is no surprise ending
That as real as ritual
Tarzan will clutch Jane's slender body
Tight in his bare, muscled arms
Tarzan's wild breath hot on Jane's face
As vine to vine they swing
Through slippery green air
Of steaming rainforests
Ahh-ee-yachhh-ee-yahhh
To where Tarzan's enchanted escarpment rises into the clouds
(Star Penis, the pygmies call it in their prayers)
Where in a land time forgot
Jane will swim naked in endless moonlight
Ahh-ee-yachhh-ee-yahhh
With that pussy-simple apeman
Jane's own inner eternal Tarzan
So, folks, the last laugh is on
That old dumb hopeless myopic motherfucker
For rearing its old hoary bald head
Once again when it shouldn't have
Again & again & again it does it
Ahh-ee-yachhh-ee-yahhh
In backseats after ballgames
In the dizzy perfume of balconies

That old ugy eye-eyed angel never learning
Its proper place
So there you have it, folks
The end of Jane's passionate moviedream of True Love
Not to mention famous flamboyant blowjob
& once again that old hapless goofy Black Lagoony creature
Will be the one to suffer
For the simple fact that time
& the passionate moviedream of True Love
Are always on the side of
The blonde & beautiful
The exquisite & escaped
Jungle Jane
Ahh-ee-yachhh-ee-yahhh

Tarzan and His Mate was the last of MGM's Tarzan series to be targeted for a strictly adult audience. The remaining MGM Tarzans, made under stricter censorship guidelines, were geared for the whole family.

At age nine, Weissmuller contracted polio. At the suggestion of his doctor, he took up swimming to help battle the disease. In the 1924 Olympics, he won five gold medals and one bronze. He won fifty-two US National Championships and set sixty-seven world records. Weissmuller starred in six Tarzan movies for MGM with actress Maureen O'Sullivan as Jane, Cheeta as his pal Chimp, and, for the last three, Johnny Sheffield as Boy. He became the definitive Tarzan and the first to be associated with the ululating, yodeling Tarzan yell, which was created by splicing together recordings of three vocalists to get the effect—a soprano, an alto, and a hog caller.

While playing in a celebrity golf tournament in Cuba in 1958, Weissmuller's golf cart was suddenly captured by rebel soldiers. Weissmuller got out of the cart and gave his trademark Tarzan yell: ahh-ee-yachhh-ee-yahhh! The socked rebels began to jump up and down cheering, "Tarzan, welcome to Cuba!" and then provided Tarzan and his companions an escort to the golf course.

For his contributions to the motion picture industry, Tarzan has a star on the Hollywood Walk of Fame at 6541 Hollywood Boulevard in Hollywood.

In 1979, after suffering a series of strokes, Tarzan entered The Motion Picture & Television Country Home and Hospital in Woodland Hills, California, where Tarzan regularly frightened the other elderly residents by wandering through the halls while calling out for Jane and his jungle friends: ahh-ee-yachhh-ee-yahhh, and at the graveside service in Acapulco, as Tarzan's coffin was lowered into the ground a tape recording of his yell was played full volume three times:

Ahh-ee-yachhh-ee-yahhh
Ahh-ee-yachhh-ee-yahhh
Ahh-ee-yachhh-ee-yahhh

B
HIGH SIERRA

HIGH SIERRA (1941) is an early heist film noir written by W.R. Burnett and John Houston and directed by Raoul Walsh. The movie features Ida Lupino and Humphrey Bogart full of hardboiled vitality as Mad Dog Roy Earle, a complex human being, a former farm boy turned mobster, a gunman who can befriend a mongrel dog (Pard) and goes out of his way to help a crippled girl, and who finally only wants freedom for himself. The film is notable as the breakthough in Bogart's screen career, leading to a sucession of critically acclaimed iconic roles that were box office hits. At the time the film was noted to have everything a gangster film should: speed, excitement, suspense, and that ennobling suggestion of futility which makes for irony and pity, with the perfect epilogue in which the gangster dies rather than surrenders.

ANOTHER STAR KISSED GOODBYE
(Poem with Gunmoll, Getaway Car, Camel or Lucky Strike, and Closeup)

The gangster crashes his way out
Of the can into the illusion of a new life
On the lam from the law & the Lord
The gangster goes wild running through the badlands
Cactus & sand of Death Valley
The gangster goes gushy at a cheap motor court
Over a crippled blonde babe with big blues
After a hard bitten
Lifetime of despair & desperation
A gangster with a heart of gold
The gangster & his gunmoll played
By a lovely, luscious young Ida Lupino
Are too hot & heavy traveling together
That motel clerk had already spotted them
Thanks to their front page fame & even little Pard
Their outlaw puppy, has his mug in the paper
Bogie belted the clerk, locked him in a closet
Bogie would drive on into LA for his cut alone
Ida would escape by bus
They would meet up later, disguise themselves
Somehow, settle in a small town
Somewhere in the middle of America
Raise a family, live on the lam forever
If it came to that
For some quick cash instead
Bogie sticks up a store in broad daylight
Bogie makes the inevitable gangster getaway pell-mell
Over dusty backcountry roads
There is a dizzy spinout & crash
There is a mad scramble
Up a rocky mountainside
Only to be cornered by swarming coppers
In the High Sierra cliffs like
A rat in a hole
Or stillborn in a birth canal
Gunfire from the coppers' gats
Exploding like popcorn in a heavy iron skillet & poured
Into an old brown grocery bag
Greasy & secret
To sneak into the drive-in movie
So this is the way
This gangster flick ends, Bogie
Firing up a final Camel (or probably Lucky Strike)
(Medium shot) reflects

Sizing up his dire gangster getaway situation
His gangster grin tight
Ironic in a closeup
Though not really in despair
So do not pity the poor gangster
For Bogie is weary of it all
Being on the lam is no life
A price on your head
The constant fear
Of being fingered
The constant fear of being shot down
Like a mad dog in the street
Or walking unaware out of a Chicago movie house
With a foreign woman wearing a red dress
Nowhere finally to turn
For solace, for grace
For the love of God
The end of the alley, curtains
For the gangster man
Sacrificial & sad in his sentimentality
Sacramental in his ritual role
Of redemption
Bitter within the hard approximation
Of justice confused
With the fate of stars
Like gods who eat themselves
Alive, Red Giants devouring
Themselves as they fulfill their fates
To burn brightly & devolve
Into White Dwarfs who dance off the stage
At the end of that vaudeville called
The universe
Just another star kissed goodbye
Imploding before our eyes into
A black hole from which
No light can ever escape
The gangster only longs at last
For his human heart to stop beating hopefully
The gangster prays to snap his fingers & vanish into the bright light of dawn
& for his burning star to come to rest at last
A star only half seen anyway, or seen for merely a moment
Out of the corner of the audience's eye
A remote viewing at most
A star only of the mind, an apparition
Of flame & flickering fame
The gangster has always felt most
Alive anyway in the imagination
Of his audience

The gangster longs to touch her hair just one more time
The gangster longs to feel this way about his gunmoll forever
Over & over again
A being of light & projection
The gangster feels the unbearable mass of absence most
A gangster with no eyewitness
Is only black space, a vacuum of nothingness
An abyss from which no cry for pity can rise
There are just two kinds of death for a spectral gangster
Sooner or later
With an empty sealed box to bury
During a starless night
There is no celestial navigation
For a gangster ghost

2

ANCIENT GANGSTER DREAM
(Poem with Screen Door, Primitive Chanting Preacher, Circling Black Shadows, and
Dying Mother's Screams)

& all last night, while the lawdogs waited armed
In the forests below, Bogie
Freezing in the zero High Sierra darkness
Had curled childlike
About his last dreams
Fearful dreams but his own dreams
Dreaming himself born
His dying mother's screams
The July sun burning into the tarpaper roof
The bumping of flies against the screen door
A primitive chanting preacher
The huge black shadows that had circled relentlessly
For three days about the coal camp
Finally Bogie had dreamed for a last time
His ancient gangster dreams
Of jobs & shootouts & getaways &
Of gory gangster deaths
Bullet ridden, leaking
The last closeup
The last words
Bubbling from Bogie's dying lips like a cartoon balloon
Of blood, Mother of God
Is this the last
Of Mad Dog Roy Earl?
Bubbling from Bogie's dying movie star
Lips, a blood bubble of ancient
Gangster prayer
Father, why hast Thou bugged out on
Your only begotten gangster, Your own
Mad Dog Roy Earl?

ANCIENT GANGSTER GRIN OF REGRET
(Poem with High Gleaming Granite Cliffs, Bullet with Number on It, Cheap Irony,
and Lawdogs Armed to the Teeth)

How
Did I ever get my movie star butt
In this grade-B black & white bullshit
To begin with? Bogie reflects, flicking
Another fag out into the cold
High Sierra morning air
They wanted Raft to begin with
Agents, Bogie reflects, producers
Assholes
In a slow pan
Down the steep, rocky mountainside
Bogie watches the early morning light
Begin to glisten on the granite cliffs
To shine bluish from the firs far below
Where the armed law waits with a bullet
With Bogie's number on it
I hope I don't piss
Or shit myself when I eat
That hot lead, Bogie reflects
I hope mine
Ain't a kicking, snapping, foamy
Gangster death
The gangster only longs now
To be down from this mountain of doom
Bogie reflects upon the ironic poetry of following
His own fresh footprints
& traces of feathertips down through the snow
Of the mountainside
The gangster picking his way, armed & dangerous, among clouds
Transparent as angels with wings of transcendent forms
Wings of snowflakes & frozen fearful breath
The gangster falling like a cruciform shadow
Over the snow & rocky grimace
Of the mountain's skull
Now if I was a fancy Dan like little Freddy Astaire
I could just fox-trot my ass out of this low-rent gangster flick
Hell, I could have been a hoofer
I could have been a song & dance man

Here at the end of the movie Bogie admits
Everything, spills the beans, rats
Himself out. Cops a plea. Bogie
Owns up at last to his final movie star
Gangster great sin, that
Attitude whose name is Cheap
Irony. Bogie acknowledges that
Ancient movie star gangster
Regret for all his lost
Chances as a cheap movie star gangster
For true American movie
Martyrdom
As a heroic shot soldier. Or sailorboy drowning
In dreamtime & baptismal belief
A philosophical, worldweary Bogie
In the final
Frames of this last gangster flick
Reflects that at least the lawdogs could never
Nail him for that capital
Crime whose name is
Anonymity

THE BIG KISSOFF

Bogie hears the barking
Faintly at first, then suddenly near
As little Pard, that cute gangster puppy
Races on cue crazily
Up the steep, rocky slope toward
That outlaw whose name
Is Death
Bogie flicks his last fag into the cold
Mountain air. Bogie knows
This is the big kissoff
Bogie steps out now to the edge of the cliff
To look for little Pard, exposing himself
To the deadly waiting aim
Of that lawdog sniper
Who has made his way above Bogie's
Hideout hoping to get just
Such a clean shot as this
To end the movie on schedule
Sometimes I go around pitying myself
Like a punk, Bogie reflects
As Bogie waits patiently at the edge of that cliff
For all of gangster death
Where in the eternity of those final
Movie moments Bogie's Mad
Dog Roy Earl movie corpse
Will forever fall
Freely in those endless frames

Bounce & roll like credits
To the bottom
Of Bogie's movie gangster
Star doom

Bogie's movie corpse will slide ninety feet down the mountainside to his just reward.
Bogie's stunt double Buster Wiles bounced a few times going down the mountain and
Wanted to do another take to do better. Forget it, said Raoul Walsh. It's good enough
For the twenty-five-cent customers. Wiles, playing Bogie's Mad Dog Roy Earl's movie
Corpse, had his hand filled with biscuits to encourage Pard to lick Roy's movie corpse
Hand for that extra pinch of pathos. Pard was erroneously rumored to be the canine
Actor Terry who played Toto in The Wizard of Oz. In fact, it was Bogart's then-pet
Zero that appears in High Sierra as Pard

Sometimes I go around pitying myself, Bogie
Reflects, & all the time
I am being carried
On great ghost wings
Into the giant night sky of stars
Star light
Star bright
Last star I see tonight
I wish I may
I wish I might
Have the wish I make this giant night

C
STAGECOACH

STAGECOACH (1939): A stagecoach sets out across the Painted Desert with a load of passengers, which includes a drunken doctor, two women, a good army wife and a whore named Dallas, played by Claire Trevor, a thieving bank manager, a Confederate cad named Hatfield, played by John Carradine, and a vengeful outlaw, the famous Ringo Kid, played by John Wayne. The trip is made incredibly dangerous and complicated by the fact that the redskin devil Geronimo is on the warpath in the area they must pass through.

GHOST RIDER
(Poem First Seen at the Palace Theater in Montgomery West Virginia, with Electric
Smoke and Brief Movie of No-Name Galaxy)

The boy is twelve years old & on Saturday
Afternoons at the Palace Theater
The boy sits in the middle
Of the very first row
So that the Western Movie fills up
Everything the boy can see
In the whole wide world
The boy is inside of the dream
Of the Western Movie
& the boy is real
For the first time in his wretched life
In all of the Western Movies
Of the boy's memory
The stagecoaches go on & on
Forever
Faster than the speed of darkness
With time folded like a dark wing into a long forever
The stagecoaches are never coming
From anyplace in particular, some
No-name galaxy in the middle of nowhere
Maybe. The stagecoaches have no special
Destinations. Some other no-name galaxy
In the middle of nowhere
Maybe. It is the stagecoach itself
Its own journey
Which is real
The stagecoaches of the boy's memory are suspended
Forever in the fluid center
Of the dream
As it dreams itself awake
In the luminosity of an eternal
Present, an enormous
Now, the immensity
Of a moment
Moving but
Motionless

In all of the Western Movie dreams
Of the boy's memory
The stagecoaches go on & on forever
The stagecoaches create their own time
Their own distances
Ghost Riders in the electric smoke
Reaching some new no-name galaxy forever
Where the boy can descend from that Ghost Rider of electric smoke
As a brand new no-name boy
At the end of his spirit journey
Unknown in a new dream
Ready to inhabit a new heroic story
Like stepping out of the dreaming cave of a black mirror
A pure reflection of electromagnetism & imagination
Enigmatic & magic
& wearing his new story like a cape made of stars & night
With a black mask to match
A being made of new stories, not old atoms
A fish dropped from the sky
By a soaring Eagle
A brave & fearless brand new desperado boy
Armed to the teeth
& dangerous
In his namelessness
& resurrection
Into the newness of a permanent
Dream

A SAD-EYED SALOON GIRL IS ABOARD
(Poem with Ugly Christian Ladies, Brick Shithouse, Milk of Mothers, Desert Light, Dust Devil, and First Boner)

A Sad-eyed Saloon Girl Babe is aboard all the stagecoaches of the boy's memory. The
Sad-eyed Saloon Girl Babe has hair the color of honey. The Sad-eyed Saloon Girl
Babe's sad eyes are blue & wide with regret & blame & she has boobs that even
At twelve years of age the boy understands won't quit. The Sad-eyed Saloon Girl Babe
Has just been run out of some God-forsaken, no-name, two-horse town by some
Really ugly Christian ladies with faces like ferrets. Who among them did ever think
They could destroy you? The Sad-eyed Saloon Girl Babe sports big bright orange
Feathers in her fancy Saloon Girl Babe bonnet, a hat she wears like a halo or sail. The
Sad-eyed Saloon Girl Babe, who even to the boy's twelve-year-old eyes is built like a
Brick shithouse, clearly has a past. But what do pasts matter to that twelve-year-old
Boy sitting in the middle of the front row at the Palace Theater who is entertaining
His first boner. Yes, this is first boner poem. What in the world is that happening
Down there with his little thingy? the boy wonders as he stares down through the
Dark to where in the depths of his drawers his little boy dick is acting very oddly
Indeed. What In The World? that boy wonders as his little worm wiggles & he
Learns to suffer invisibly. The Sad-eyed Saloon Girl Babe has flesh like silk & a face
Like glass. The boy's wide eyes pass over the flesh & face of the Sad-eyed Saloon
Girl's landscape like clouds full of tears & sperm, as he hovers on the brink of
Language capable of capturing these first feelings, at the cusp of words lovely &
Dangerous & dirty & cruel enough to say sacred things. Could this be that boy's
First wink & blink from that Fallen Mystery Angel named Love? Oh, the immensity
Of it all! The pure bitter, sad sacredness of this thing called Love! The boy's new little
Boner & heart swell as he looks deeply into the enormous blue planets & infinite
Orbits of the Sacred Saloon Girl Babe's sad, giant cinema eyes, at her wondrous
Titties full of the milk of mothers. & then the stagecoach, amid swelling music &
Electric clouds of dust in the middle of those heartless Badlands called Nowhere
Pulls up to a shape hazy as a dust devil in the holy desert light, the silhouette of a sand
Spirit, that manifests itself slowly as a handsome, steely-eyed stranger

THE HANDSOME STEELY-EYED STRANGER BESIDE THE DUSTY TRAIL
(Poem with Big Iron, Wanted Poster, Painted Desert, and Second World War)

The handsome Steely-eyed Stranger beside the dusty trail had to shoot his faithful
Albeit crippled horse, the Steely-eyed Stranger explains. Climb aboard, Steely-eyed
Stranger, the grizzled old coot of a driver says, eyeballing the Stranger's low-slung
Notched Big Iron. The Stranger sizes up each passenger with his steely-eyed gaze
The Saloon Girl Babe's wide, clear, blue, enormous, sad, sacred cinema eyes meet
The steely stare of the handsome Stranger. The Saloon Girl Babe's smile is girlish
Somehow, shy almost, & her tiny Saloon Girl Babe wrists look as delicate as glass
The steely-eyed gaze of the handsome Stranger settles upon the Saloon Girl Babe's
Bazookas. His Big Iron wiggles. The Steely-eyed Stranger grins, so confident & holy
& handsome in his horniness. This Steely-eyed Stranger clearly has a past too. He is
Mysterious & bold & superior in his secrets. Even to the boy's twelve-year-old eyes it
Is evident that this Stranger is a silent, solitary, reluctant Western Movie Hero type, a
Holy & innocent Hero type from the mythological wilderness, a Magical Warrior type
From that terrible land of freedom that exists beyond the law. Clearly the Stranger has
Shot up his share of saloons, robbed a bank or two, robbed his share of stagecoaches
In his youth riding with a Wild Bunch throughout the Old West. This Stranger has
Often come upon his own face on faded Wanted Posters tacked to cottonwoods
Down by Lonesome Wolf Creek, where he practices his quick draw relentlessly &
Masturbates in the melancholy of his essential isolation & loneliness into the mud
Amid the mounds of spent shells. But this Stranger has always tried to live truly by
His own frontier code of justice & honor & magical speed of hand with guns. This
Stranger clearly has become weary with the burden of legend & myth & struggling
With complicated questions of good & evil, his frontier code of honor eroded by
Irony & the encroachment of civilization, accepting finally with reluctance that only
The outlaw can ironically represent the myth of freedom, the only question finally
Being who deserves to live & who deserves to do the killing. The Stranger is not all
Bad though. The Stranger has never gunned a man down just to watch him snap &
Foam & gurgle, his face a fly farm before he even falls. The Stranger has never ridden
A good horse into the ground just to make a clean getaway from old regrets & that
Ancient blame for losing the farm. The Stranger is always polite to Saloon Girl pussy
It is painfully clear to the twelve-year-old boy sitting in the front row at the Palace
Theater that this handsome Steely-eyed Stranger is ready now to forsake the sweet
Anarchy of his outlaw youth for the special love of a Sad-eyed Saloon Girl Babe with
Wrists as delicate as glass & Bazooms to die & go to heaven for. Do not be afraid
When the evil Indian redskin devils, trapped in their past, attack their manifest
Destiny futilely in the form of this stagecoach (or Cowboy Bus, as the boy always
Strangely thought of these conveyances across painted deserts). Do not be afraid
When both the Old Coot driver & the Shotgun Rider are feathered with arrows &
Fall like dead angels from the stagecoach leaving the horses to run amok. The Steely-
Eyed Stranger fires his Big Iron from the narrow window relentlessly. Handsomely
He swings out of the narrow window amid a feathery futility of foolish arrows like
A savior angel. Who among those foolish redskin devils ever did think they could
Destroy him?

It occurs to the boy sitting in the front row of the Palace Theater that this handsome
Steely-eyed Stranger is a deadringer for John Wayne. The boy's own dad is a
Deadringer for John Wayne. Everybody says so. The neighbors do. The boy's own
Mom says so. The boy's own mom is beautiful. You could get lost in the ocean of
Sadness & regret in the boy's own mom's brown eyes. The boy's dad is a Hero too. The
Boy's dad pretty much won the Second World War singlehandedly. Everybody says so
The boy's dad says so. The town had a big parade for the boy's dad when he returned
Home on the train from winning the Second World War pretty much singlehandedly
The handsome Steely-eyed Stranger shoots & shoots as redskin braves bite their
Manifest destiny whose name is dust. The boy's first little boner is only a fond
Memory at this point. At this point the boy hates heroes with all of his heart. The boy
Knows that he doesn't stand a chance with no wings, no feathers
No Big Iron

On Saturday afternoons at the Palace Theater, besides the main feature & cartoons &
a news reel, they also run a serial …

MASKED MAN
(Poem with Silver Bullet, Big-Tooth Tigers, Trouble, and Condom)

The Durango Kid is the boy's favorite serial cowboy who dresses all in black &
Wears a mask, outside of Maybe Hopalong Cassidy, who wears black, or The Lone
Ranger, who wears a mask, & uses silver bullets, & has an Indian brave named Tonto
As his best friend. Most of the time he was just a regular ranch hand named Steve
Although his last name seemed to change from serial to serial, Saturday to Saturday
& Steve just rode a regular horse named Bullet, but when trouble of some kind would
Arrive in town, the stagecoach would be held up say, or some cattle rustled out on
The range, or the bank in town robbed, then regular old Steve would simply seem to
Vanish into thin air, just ride out of town all alone as though he was heading for the
Hills or something to avoid the trouble in town, but folks would claim they had seen
Regular Steve duck into one of the many old deserted mines in the hills around town
Or sometimes disappear into the dark of one of the old abandoned mines in the hills
Around town, or disappear into one of the old dreaming caves of the ancient tribes in
That part of the country, dreaming caves where the ancient ones would build fires &
Beat ceremonial drums as they chanted & worshipped the bones & skulls they found
In piles in the dreaming caves, caves with walls covered with the painted shapes &
Faces of animals long gone from the face of the Earth, big-tooth tigers, wooly coated
Bison, cave bears the size of barns & covered with the painted handprints of braves
Dead & buried for generations, & then later out would ride regular old Steve on a
Huge white stallion he called Raider, & Steve would be dressed all in black, & wearing
A black mask, as though he had disappeared into another dimension & returned as a
New man made of shadows from the dark of the dreaming cave, a new, transformed
Masked man now looking for trouble to embrace, & folks now called regular old Steve
A new name: The Durango Kid, & said that he was actually a hero behind that mask
Come back from that cave of the dead to protect & save them like a holy warrior from
Another world

The Durango Kid seemed to have black masks, & black cowboy outfits, & huge white
Stallions hidden
In every single cave of the Old West, so that at a moment's notice, regular old Steve
Could transform himself intoThe Durango Kid, who was his real, secret, heroic self, &
Almost holy in his need to protect & save people with his quickness of hand & blazing
Six-guns

The boy stashes old Halloween masks
Throughout the whole neighborhood
So that at a moment's notice
The boy can slip into a neighbor's garage, or duck behind a hedge &
Emerge masked & secret & mysterious
A masked phantom boy haunting his childhood neighborhood
A boy who is mysterious & bold & superior in his secrets, maybe even holy
The boy reinvents his life from the wretched boy he has always been
Into the bold Hero Boy he can imagine himself becoming

He is a Hero Boy who lives by his own frontier code
Of honor & justice
He is a Hero Boy who can be cruel for the sake
Of a higher goodness, but never mean nor petty nor small
The boy will find work as a Fast Gun for hire
& do the neighborhood's dirty work
With his magical speed of hand with guns
Then Ride away into the mystical Tetons wounded & bloody
His work done, never to be heard from again
Who was that Masked Magical Warrior Boy so willing
To save & protect us from evil
With such brave, bold behavior & handsomeness
& magical speed of hand with guns?
Who was that Masked Holy Hero Boy?
Why did that Masked Holy Hero Boy leave us with this here
Silver bullet? is the big question
Throughout the boy's neighborhood
The boy tosses the silvery token
Onto the porch of old mean Miss Roberts, his third grade teacher
Rings her doorbell
Ducks behind her hedge
She comes out to investigate
Old, mean Miss Roberts does
Bends over, blind as a bat
In the bright porch light
To gaze with wonder at that mysterious
Shiny silvery item left behind
On her front porch. That shiny coin of a condom
Robbed from the boy's dad's dresser drawer
When suddenly a masked Space Alien Monster From Outer Space Boy leaps out
From behind the black hedge of the giant night
At old, mean, blind-as-a-bat Miss Roberts screaming
Insanely, whereupon old mean Miss Roberts stumbles back against her front door
Clutching her throat then covers her face with her hands now that finally it is her turn
To go with them

SHITTING SHANE

Out of the pure sappy adult sentiments
Of parental pity & guilt for their deformed boy
After his third major surgery
At the famous Mayo Clinic, the Mom & the Dad
For his tenth birthday
Present the tragic boy with a profound mystery
A Magic Movie Machine!!!!
A Magic Movie Projector
With a four-minute Woody Woodpecker cartoon
& one eight-minute Western Movie
Starring Hopalong Cassidy, dressed all in black
Blazing silvery six-gun pistols as he gallops across the Western Movie World
The boy plays the Western Movie over & over until
The projector is warm to his touch, hot even
& seems to glow
Projecting the holy, electric light
A magic window against his darkened bedroom wall
The boy looks out onto the Western Movie World
He watches Hopalong Cassidy ride his huge white
Stallion silently across the shimmering Western Movie World completely
At the boy's will. If the boy messes around with the Magic Movie
Projector
The boy can slow the Western Movie down or speed
The Western Movie
Up. The boy can make the Western Movie run
Backwards
With smoke returning
Like imploding ghosts to gun
Barrels & dead men falling
Upwards into life again

If the boy gets bored with the Western
Movie he can use the holy projected
Electric light to make hand
Shadows on his bedroom
Wall, the heads
Of huge rabbits, big black birds
Carnivorous crows, ravenous
Ravens, Woody Woodpecker giants
Creatures from the boy's dreams, terrible &
Purely imaginary, tigers, trolls, demons, an animal
Imagined by Poe, a minotaur
A creature with the unfolded wings
Of a bird, & the tail of a fish, that changes with sleep
& wakefulness, Swedenborg's devils
Who can eat their way solemnly
Across the Western
Movie at the boy's will, masticating Hopalong, The
Lone Ranger, The Durango Kid, Billy
The Kid, Paladin, The Ringo Kid, & completely
At the boy's leisure
Shitting Shane

D
THE MOLLY MAGUIRES

THE MOLLY MAGUIRES (1970) stars Sean Connery as Black Jack Kehoe, the union organizer and leader of The Molly Maguires, a secret organization of Irish coal miners established in the 19th century to fight oppressive mine owners, and Richard Harris as James McParlan, the company spy disguised as an undercover Irish poet type packed with the postures of pain and philosophy. Set in late 19th century Northeastern Pennsylvania, this social drama tells the story of an undercover detective sent to a coal mining community to expose the Molly Maguires, who coldly betrays the group whose leader he has befriended.

1

SOMETIMES POETS ARRIVE IN TOWN ON TRAINS FROM PITTSBURGH LATE AT NIGHT INCOGNITO

(Poem with Soundtrack by Henry Mancini, Employing Irish Modal Harmony, Played by Period Instruments Including the Irish Harp, Penny Whistle, and Squeezebox)

Poets may be unprepossessing in appearance
Wearing, say, a simple, threadbare suit
A soft, slouch cap, a bowtie
Perfect strangers, poets gravitate
Toward the warm lights
Of the lone tavern in town
Looking for the company of working men
New best friends & comrades
& information to use to send
These new best friends & comrades
To the gallows
Poets appear to be friendly enough
If somewhat shy
Poets give short answers
To questions
Poets cultivate an air of mystery
Poets pretend that they have something
To hide
Which they do of course
Only not what they pretend
They do
Poets are capable of kicking
Some serious ass. Poets have quick hands
Soft or not
Poets fight dirty. Poets gouge eyes & kick
Their opponents in the balls
Or teeth
If given half the chance
Poets don't go down easily
Poets get back up again & again
Poets gain grudging respect
Which is the first step
Toward trust
Which is finally
All that Poets live for
Poets appear to care
Poets appear to be tenderhearted
Poets can carry a tune
Poets sing lovely, old Irish ballads

Poets have handsome if somewhat battered
Faces. Poets have essentially sad
Faces, & sensuous
Sensitive mouths & eyes as blue
As bruises
Poets are soulful
Poets look like spies, which is what they essentially are
Poets pull their weight underground
Working with their miner brothers
In the dark. Walking home after a hard dayshift
Down in the hole, Poets stop to play ball
With boys in the muddy street. It seems to be always
About to rain or raining in the sad, grim
Tragic little town, which was saved from demolition because of the movie being set
There, & made into a mining museum, whose dripping dark houses depress
The spirits of the Poet
& force the Poet to reflect upon
How essentially lonely the Poet is
Poets brood over their beers
Late into the night at the tavern. Poets appear
To have a lot to forget. Poets appear to be full
Of regret. Poets appear to understand the nature
Of loss. Poets can hold their booze
Poets have a way with words
But Poets hide in what they say
Poets are devious & honest
Equally. Poets tell true lies
In their eternal struggle
To keep their stories straight
Poets come to believe totally in everything
They make up
Poets are charming. Poets are romantic
Poets take their girls
On romantic picnics in the woods
Poets entertain their girls, the lovely Miss Mary Raines in this case, played by the
Lovely Samantha Eggar, with touching
Funny stories about childhoods
They never had. Poets are well-read
Poets impress their girls
With memorized poems. Poets say enigmatic things
To their girls like
I envy you your morality & that's the truth. But you can buy decency &
The law like a loaf of bread
Poets remain riddles to their girls
Poets are great kissers

2
POETS NEVER GET ENOUGH
(Poem with Capital Punishment)

Poets thrive on rebellion
Poets get caught up in
Rebellion's wonder & excitement
A Poet must become more like his enemy
Than his enemy is
Finally Poets
Cannot fake
All of their feelings
Poets must come to truly love & join
What they are set upon betraying
Poets must believe that they live charmed lives
& that they will never deserve to die
Poets are beyond dreams of redemption
Poets are philosophical
Poets appreciate the beauty of the sacrificial impulse
Finally what poets seek is forgiveness
Even love, from those they have betrayed
Awaiting execution, Black Jack Kehoe tells his erstwhile friend & ally McParlan
Whom he has come to love like a brother, that no punishment short of Hell can
Redeem his treachery. McParlan retorts that, In that case, I'll see you in Hell
Punishment is what poets truly seek
Poets never get enough
Poets dream of the smoke of dragons
To ride from town
To town
Mere rings of mortal bone
Sometimes Poets wander into the woods alone armed
With a loaded pistol
Never to be seen alive again
Did we say that Poets are great kissers?
Poets never get enough

INVASION OF THE BODY SNATCHERS

INVASION OF THE BODY SNATCHERS (1956) is a thrilling, disturbing classic science fiction/alien invasion film that was precisely executed and packed with action by director Don Seigel.

The story depicts an extraterrestrial invasion of a small Californian town, in which alien invaders replace human beings with duplicates disgorged from seed pods as the human beings sleep and dream away their last moments fully alive on Earth before they are transformed into mobile beans, or pod-people. The duplicates appear identical in outward appearance but are devoid of any emotion or individuality. A local General Practitioner, Dr. Miles Bennell, played to a T by Kevin McCarthy, struggles to stop the alien invaders dead in their tracks, such as they are.

Doctor Kevin returns innocently enough to his hometown from a medical convention only to be informed by his faithful nurse that many of his regular patients and other townspeople are acting oddly. They don't appear to be their regular old selves, as though they have changed their essential identities, or else something otherworldly and perchance even evil has taken possession of them. On the other hand, perhaps it is simply a case of mass hysteria in which everybody in town is suffering from the strange delusion that whenever somebody falls asleep an exact replica of them will be born from these giant seed pods that have strangely appeared all over town, and the best guess is that there is an alien menace in their small, quiet town that propagates itself when a person is asleep and he or she is duplicated and replaced by a zombie-like other-self born from the pods from outer space. Doctor Kevin finds himself with many questions, but few answers. Doctor Kevin's best friend Jack discovers an odd cadaverlike creature lying on his pool table with an unfinished, half formed face like the first impression that's stamped on a coin that isn't finished, as though the creature is simply taking a little nap. Later this repugnant corpse turns into an exact replica of Jack, awakens, flutters its gooey eyes, and opens a beer.

On a premonition that his love interest, Becky Driscoll, played by Dana Wynter, is in danger, Doctor Kevin races to her house, which he enters through a basement window, where he finds a replica double for Dana hidden in a bin, obviously by her zombiefied father. Doctor Kevin decides to host a neighborhood barbecue at his house to clear the air, where, in the famous greenhouse scene, Doctor Kevin and Dana discover among rotting cabbages a pod giving birth to a regular person replica amid milky, gooey fluid that bubbles out around the disgorged human being counterpart, which in turn is covered with a sticky, sappy foam, whereupon Kevin grabs a handy pitchfork and stabs the pod-person in the heart as though it were a mere vampire, another, more regular species of the undead. So, yes, clearly there is an alien menace in their quiet town, perhaps as the result of atomic radiation on some distant planet's plant life, turning it into some weird alien race of turnips governed by some primal instinct not utterly unlike the basic human instinct that governs the formation of flesh and blood out of thin air from fucking.

When Warner Studio scheduled three previews for the film before its general release, they discovered that the audiences could not follow the film and laughed in the wrong places. In response, the studio removed much of the film's humor, plus humanity and quality, according to Siegel, and from then on it became a studio policy not to mix humor with horror, and more's the pity. Many theaters, including the Palace Theater in the Boy's hometown, displayed several of the pods (made of paper) in their lobbies and entrances along with large, lifelike, black and white cutouts of Doctor Kevin and the lovely Dana running frantically away from a crowd of advancing townspeople. The boy had petted one of the pods like a stray puppy he had found and could take home to raise as his own personal pet pod, and perhaps teach tricks, like to roll over and to beg for treats and to play dead, or turn it into his own Dad on command who would shuffle around the house slowly like a zombie, and would leave the boy alone and never get angry and scream and yell or hit the boy if the boy got close enough to grab. The boy thought that Dana Wynter was the most beautiful woman he had ever seen, more beautiful even than his saloon-girl goddess. Dana had milky white shoulders and short, black hair.

Years later when the boy met Rainy McCall, it occurred to him that she could have been Dana's daughter, or Dana's twin sister even, and that Dana could have easily been Rainy's movie double or starred in a movie about Rainy's life. And that last night on the farm during that terrible thunderstorm, when he saw Rainy running frantically through the apple trees of the old orchard on the hill, he recalled vividly Dana running through the hills above town for her life, and stopped to watch at the edge of the orchard for zombielike pod-people stumbling after Rainy as they dripped goo and afterbirth.

THE NARROW ESCAPE OF CHILDHOOD SWEETHEARTS
(Poem with Puppy, Old Cave Creatures Long Extinct, and Dreaming Bats)

The childhood sweethearts
Dana & Doctor Kevin
Were finally the only two people left
In their small town
Who were their true selves
Dana & Doctor Kevin tried to make a clean getaway
From that place
The trick to this
Was to appear dreamy & serene
To walk along the street slowly & not show emotion one
When a little puppy was almost run over
In the middle of Main Street
Dana screamed
Showing emotion one

The townspeople turned upon Dana & Doctor Kevin
The last two true people
Who made their escape into the hills
Dana & Doctor Kevin ran & ran until
They thought their human hearts would burst
Dana & Doctor Kevin collapsed into one another's arms
Deep within an old abandoned Indian cave
They had explored as kids
Dana & Doctor Kevin clutched one another in the dark
They listened to the shouts outside of the torch-bearing townspeople
From somewhere deeper in the cave
Water dripped
Like tiny heartbeats
Or the dream drums of ancient Indians as they chanted & prayed
& prepared to dream the old cave animals back to life
There was the scurrying of little feet
Rustlings along black walls
Sounds like faint sighs
Sounds like the soft breath
Of dreaming bats

THE LAST CHANCE TO DIE FOR LOVE
(Poem with Magic Ring, Mushroom Race, Cave Bear Skull, Cold Lips, Mask of
Invisibility, and Dripping Afterbirth)

Perhaps the last two true people
Should keep moving
Make that perilous dream journey
Deeper & deeper into the ancient Indian dreaming
Cave, wait patiently in the dark
For deliverance into another dimension
Slip through some magic ring
Into another realm
Hide out, secret, on the lam far from the surface
Of their old true lives forever
Memories of their old world of light
Fading away slowly
Like some dim, lost dream
Of childhood
Fold themselves
Into a last family, give birth to
Some sort of lost, lustrous-eyed
Mushroom race
In the dark of the dreaming cave
The light of day
A lost dream to be yearned toward
All they would have to do
Is lay low & stay awake
For the rest of their natural lives
For if either of them
Either Dana or Doctor Kevin
Fell asleep to dream for even a single moment
Their alien movie doubles would take their places
In the world
& their own true selves
Would drift off as though their own true selves
Had been no more than apparitions or the shadows of dreams
Upon the face of the Earth

Doctor Kevin collects some stuff for fuel from the front of the cave & builds a small
Fire in a cave bear skull. In the flickering light of the flames Doctor Kevin & Dana
Study the painted shapes & faces of cave creatures on the cave walls gone a thousand
Years. That girl, Dana says to Doctor Kevin. That girl you were making love to my last
Dream on Earth. She looked like me, almost exactly like me. Like a double of me in
Some horror movie version of my life

Doctor Kevin and Dana's human destiny unfolds finally when Doctor Kevin returns
From scouting around the vast maze
Of abandoned mines & caves
The dark, dizzying labyrinth
Of their new inner life together
To discover Dana
With her beautiful, dark eyes
Closed tight
Doctor Kevin clutches Dana up into his arms
Her crow black hair so fragrant
In Doctor Kevin's breath
The white skin of Dana's throat
So soft
This woman Doctor Kevin would die for
When Doctor Kevin kisses Dana's cold lips
Dana opens blank, alien eyes
Doctor Kevin sees his reflection dead
In those dark eyes of dazzling flatness
It is all that Doctor Kevin had really expected. Dreaming cave or not, at some point
Dana would fall asleep & suddenly be gone, lost in her own dark dreams, the light
Gone forever from her dark eyes like the last flicker of a Western sunset, just vanished
Gone, except for her lovely body
Doctor Kevin knows at once
He has just lost his last chance
To die for love now
In what is left of his tragic
Human lifetime

THE LAST EGG OF LOVE

After emptying the cave bear skull he had used to build their final fire of ashes Doctor
Kevin positions it back on the cave floor among the piles of bones & rests Dana's head
gently upon it like a pillow, beneath the painted face of a cave bear
For protection. He folds Dana's arms over her beautiful breasts as though she is
Embracing herself for warmth, or embracing her inner alien, it occurs to Doctor
Kevin. It also occurs to him that beans don't have breasts, beautiful or otherwise, &
More's the pity. Doctor Kevin adjusts the old shaman bear mask he had found hidden
Deep in the cave over his face, which will make him invisible, & he settles the bear
Hair cape he also found over his shoulders, which will enable him to fly through time
Like a handsome spirit animal, & talk to the dead. Doctor Kevin kisses Dana lightly
On her cold lips & says: Now I lay you down to sleep, I pray your soul the Lord will
Keep, but if you should die
Before you wake, I pray your soul the Lord will take. Then Doctor Kevin stands erect
& shuffles like a giant bean, dripping & gooey with his own afterbirth, which he leaves
Behind him like the sticky trail of a snail but as invisible as a shadow in a dark cave
Toward the entrance without expectation or hope

I am only recently returned from the dreaming of the star cave, Doctor Kevin says
As he shuffles among
The ambivalent aliens on the hillside
Like a cave-blind creature of sperm
An unborn relic left on the grave of moonlight
I am returned to rub my feathered wings in song
Unsheltered in the new night
Under a wilderness of strange stars
Silver in moonlight
Glass in moonlight, transparent but shining
Like a mirror
I am not one of you
But I am not myself
Please forgive my inexactness
The world is not familiar to whom I am not
This rendezvous with a parallel reality
The lost dream of my love has been drained, you see
But I carry with me my love's last egg
Harvested in the moonlight of the star cave
Where the future comes to you in dreams
I am the wings of my love's last egg
You may take the body of my love but
You cannot take my love's last egg

Whereupon Doctor Kevin sees his love there among the aliens on the hillside
Her lovely face serene in torchlight
& he says to her
Let us sit in the warm summer rain of the cave once more & sing with emotion
Let me see you dance once again
& time will begin once more
For both the world of the aliens & for our own kind
Now Doctor Kevin leads Dana's movie double toward the entrance
Of the star cave & its dreams of the future
Her face now streaming with tears
The aliens fall away from them
Making a path for their dream journey
Back to the beginning of their home-poem
Where they were first imagined

F
THE ROMANCES OF RAINY MCCALL:
TRAGIC WANTON HIPPIE PRINCESS FROM THE LOST AGE OF AQUARIUS
OR
THE OLD SORCERER'S DAUGHTER

THE ROMANCES OF RAINY MCCALL (1979) is an early Jim Jarmusch film from his final year at NYU, shot under the tutelage of renowned film noir director Nicholas Ray. Upon showing Ray the script, Ray expressed his disappointment in its lack of action, to which Jarmusch responded by reworking the script to be even less eventful in the manner and mode of Joseph Cornell. Jarmusch was the only student Ray hired as a personal assistant to work on Lightning Over Water, Ray's documentary about his dying years, on which he was collaborating with Wim Wenders. NYU, unimpressed by Jarmusch's senior project, in which he'd inserted scenes from favorite old black and white classics such as Tarzan and His Mate, High Sierra, Stagecoach, Invasion of the Body Snatchers, Forbidden Planet, Creature from the Black Lagoon, Attack of the Crab Monsters, Captain Blood, and Mary of Scotland, and added a new soundtrack featuring the Grateful Dead and Jefferson Airplane, along with Janis Joplin and Big Brother and the Holding Company, refused to award Jarmusch a degree. Jarmusch responded in The Golden Rules of Filming and Poetry: Nothing is original. Steal from anywhere that resonates with inspiration or fuels your imagination. Devour old films, new films, music, books, paintings, photographs, poems, dreams, random conversations, architecture, bridges, street signs, trees, clouds, bodies of water, light and shadows. Select only things to steal from that speak directly to your soul. If you do this, your work (and theft) will be authentic. Authenticity is invaluable; originality is nonexistent. And don't bother concealing your thievery—celebrate it if you feel like it. In any case, always remember what Jean-Luc Godard said: It's not where you take things from—it's where you take them to.

GHOST HOLO-SIGNALS FROM THE TRAGIC DECADES OF BLURRY BLACK AND WHITE TELEVISION
(Poem with Christmas Lights, Trade Winds, and Hooker)

For the first giant night in a week
The trade winds are blowing
Hot & sweet through the bar's open windows
The big banyan tree overhead
Sighs & shakes ghostly limbs lit year round with
Christmas lights
In relief
Like the
Shivery wings of an angel of unnatural acts named Rainy McCall weeping over spilt
Life
Tears & foamy sperm
Dripping from her chin like
An insouciance of surf
Ghost signals
As they called them back in the tragic decades
Of blurry black & white television
Surf such as a melancholy old sailor named Joe Harris
Only recently coughed up on these final shores
Had floated in earlier on this tropical island Christmas afternoon
Masturbating like a form
Of meditation or maybe prayer
About the mystery & mythic narrative of Rainy's own old black & white movie, & his
Supporting role
In it

Now Joe Harris lingers in an obscure corner
Of his life on the lam from
Love
In a barroom glowing as soft & sinister as the inside of an old radio
Its tubes flickering to death with pale yellow light

Joe Harris kills time watching the big, brand new colored television set & small
Salt water aquarium
Behind
The bar
As silvery wings of bubbles shiver toward the surface to vanish like breath
When Slim, a star hooker in tight, magenta
Synsilk shorts, cools into the Café Sleezo
From the uneasy menance of the alley darkness

In the trick of neon
Slim's magenta shorts weave
An afterglow of a pale, sea green shark shadow
Across the tiny tank behind the bar
On this giant night of pirated privacy for Joe Harris
On the lam from LA, city
Of lost angels & light &
Projection, on
A wing & a bad check
For a cheap motel room hideout with slippery green mold on the shower walls, & an
Old blurry black & white teevee
For Joe Harris
On this one giant night especially
In the interlunar lull
The giant night of the month when the Pisces moon maiden
Is perfectly invisible
The trades
Just now kicking in
The whole island scary & electric with it
Winds as hot & sweet as Rainy's salty
Surf breath
This anniversary giant night
Of Joe Harris's interstellar teardrop slowdance
From years back, back in the tragic decades
Of blurry black & white television when Rainy McCall
Took her final spacewalk, floating free
From the gravity of life.
Waltzing with her wily, wanton wisdom
Off to a new satellite of love
Somewhere over the sleeping volcanoes of Hawaii
Leaving Joe Harris & Angst
Their whining pooch
To watch the past ripple away from the rock splash of Rainy's departure
On the illuminated LA motel pool's baby blue waves

Lovely, high-cheeked, mystery Mongolian face
Dark & shiny, short, outerspace punked hair
A tiny ruby earring glimmering like Mars
Hey Joe Harris, sez the star hooker Slim
To Joe Harris, you want some company, man?

2

UNDERCOVER ASTRONAUT MAN:
THE SECRET AGENDA OF THE AMERICAN SPACE PROGRAM
(Installation Poem with Bikini Panties, Plump Planets, and Golf on the Moon)

Wilma Sue sets a bone white cup down before what is left
Of Joe Harris, a mysterious stranger clearly hungover, shaky
& forlorn, pours in coffee hot & black as the blood of trolls
Fluorescent lights caught like tiny constellations in its dark, rich flow
Baseball cap pulled low over his gummy midnight movie spooky eyes
Joe Harris observes Wilma Sue's lacy, black bikini panties
Beneath her pale blue nylon uniform
Joe Harris observes Wilma Sue's lovely Scotch-Irish arms
White & milky, clusters of real kissable freckles
Sprinkled like little, lickable sunspots amid the fine blonde babe fuzz
Reading the mind of Joe Harris like a dirty book without a cover
Wilma Sue sez, I can't stand the sun
It burns me right up. I'm a lady what loves the night
Wilma Sue puts down the coffee pot & presses
Sausages shaped like tiny penises on the grill
Joe Harris sips his hot black troll blood, observes Wilma Sue
Observes her black bikini panties shift
Beneath the pale blue nylon like an astronomer
Might trace the movement of plump planets in orbit
& if all plump planets in orbit moved like that
Joe Harris would be on an early spaceship out
Need anything else, honey? sez Wilma Sue
When Joe Harris sops the last drops of his sunnyside-up eggs
Wilma Sue's Scotch-Irish eyes are blue
Joe Harris cannot help from observing
Blue, blue eyes drawing Joe Harris in like the image
Of a tropical lagoon might on late night, color television
The overhead fluorescents reflecting
On the rippling surfaces of those blue lagoony eyes
Joe Harris longs to spread out & float
On the rippling waters of those blue lagoony eyes
Like you might spread out & float in the rippling blue light
Of late night, color television

To tell the whole truth, sez Joe Harris to Wilma Sue
What I need right now ain't hardly that legal
& I ought to know
As I am a lawyer man. I am a doctor man too
I am a senator's son. I am the brother
Of Marlon Brando. I am an Indian chief
I am currently an undercover astronaut man on vacation
I have played golf on the moon
What are you doing after work, dear? & what time, dear, do you get off?
Wilma Sue leans across the counter closer to Joe Harris
Her big tropical lagoony blue eyes wide & bright
Now that's my big secret, sez Wilma Sue, winking & blinking
Her big blues to beat the band

MIDNIGHT MOVIES
(Poem as Still Life with Radio and Oldies but Goodies by Elvis and Bobby Vinton)

What is that other blue memory Joe Harris endlessly reruns
In the midnight movies of his mind
Blue, blue, blue
That thin, bright blue river of ionized mercury vapor particles joyride memory
Stretching across the Illinois interstate flatness toward Peoria
Joe Harris & Rainy McCall joyriding on into that blue river of mercury vapor filling
The dark, rushing interior of the old Ford
As if they were destined to drown in that blue river of mercury vapor
& the soft blue of the dashboard lights, & the glowing, ancient Elvis blue suede shoes
Radio
With Rainy singing along
Whereupon Bobby Vinton crooning Blue Velvet comes on the radio
& Rainy commences to sing along to that old tune too
Destined to fill up their lungs with blue electromagnetic waves & die together

& speaking of still life as an art genre, said Charlie Trout ...

Poem Note to Be Narrated by Resonating Radio Announcer Voice in the Manner of Orson Welles Broadcasting The War of the Worlds over the Old Silvertone Mystery Radio We Bought for Maybe Five Bucks at the Goodwill Down on Mission Street

Petrus Christus' portrait of a bride & groom visiting a goldsmith is a typical example of a transitional still life depicting both religious & secular content, though mostly allegorical in message. Caravaggio applied his influential form of naturalism to still life. One of Rembrandt's rare still life paintings, Little Girl with Dead Peacocks, is a sympathetic female portrait with images of death. Especially popular were vanitas paintings in which sumptuous arrangements of fruit or flowers were accompanied by symbolic reminders of life's impermanence, such as a skull, an hourglass, a pocket watch, a candle burning down, or the grin on the corpse of a gangster.
Cezanne found in still life the perfect vehicle for his revolutionary explorations in geometric spatial organization. In Joan Miró's still life paintings, objects appear weightless & float in lightly suggested two-dimensional space, & even mountains are drawn as simple lines. With a combination of realism & Cubist-derived abstraction, Georgia O'Keeffe's ultrarealistic closeup flower paintings reveal both the physical structure & the emotional & sexual subtext of petals as pussies. In Mexico, Frida Kahlo created her own brand of Surrealism, featuring native foods full of passion or poison, & Aztec motifs like masks of the sacrificial dead torn from the faces of severed heads bounced like bloody balls down the stone stairs of the pyramidal temples of savage gods in her still life paintings packed with personal pain & myth. Much pop art is based on still life. Roy Lichtenstein's Still Life with Goldfish Bowl combines the pure colors of Matisse with the pop iconography of Warhol. The Neo-Dada movement, including Jasper Johns, returned to Duchamp's three-dimensional representation of everyday household objects to create their own brand of still life work.

Alfred E. Neuman, *Still Life: A History*, trans. Melvin Furd (New York: Harry N. Abrams, 1999), 71-72.

(Is there a hidden poem submerged like a secret message in the previous passage or what?)

44

ESCAPE VELOCITY
(Poem with Patio, Starship, and Tall Frosty Highball, Wherein the Undercover
Astronaut Is on the Verge of Getting Laid)

Joe Harris calls the number on the napkin note
23 Elm Road is this silvery satellite/space capsule affair that has fallen from its orbit
A fallen starship cleverly disguised to look not unlike
A shiny aluminum-skinned Airstream trailer
Up on cinderblocks, amid a well trimmed little yard with blue flowers
The smell of burning charcoal, smoke drifting
Up into the fast fading evening light
Wilma Sue on a chaise longue on the little back patio
Sipping a tall white frosty highball
Hi, rocketman, sez Wilma Sue, see you found the joint
How bout a tall frosty highball to cool your heels?
Easy on the tonic, sez Joe Harris
The tall frosty highball hits the spot
The steaks are done to a medium rare turn
The evening air smells like fresh mown grass
After a summer rain
The evening air smells like the mystery musk of Rainy's damp skin
After she has made love on a hot August afternoon
Imagine if you would, folks
The crushed roses scent of Rainy's underarms
Those tropical Edens of original scents & endless surprise
Or the same scent of her slick inner thighs
Those special, secret, tropical places
We all lived to lick back in that lost age
Of electric hair & flowers
The evening sky above the little patio
Turns tropical pink, thin shifting shades of rosy light
On the lower curves of the clouds
Where rain is born
Like the neon glow of late night, color television
On the tan flesh of Rainy's long, smooth legs
On the slopes of her hips & shadowy shoulders
On her sleeping, secret face
The silvery skin of the fallen starship glows with sunset
Like the rosy ghost reflections of a dying star
The moon rises like a pale projection of itself
At a drive-in movie

I bet you all never did really go up there on that old moon, sez Wilma Sue
Wilma Sue pushes back Joe Harris's long blonde hair
I played golf up there on that moon I swear it, sez Joe Harris
I am just on vacation from my important government work
As an undercover astronaut man, sez Joe Harris
Wilma Sue kisses Joe Harris soft on his sad lips
Wilma Sue unbuttons Joe Harris's shirt tender & slow
I longed to change my lowdown life, sez Joe Harris, I longed to blast off to other
Worlds
Escape velocity is what I longed for

THE SOFT BLUE SUEDE GRAVITY OF LOVE
(Poem with Fold-Out Bed and Body Parts)

The lives of astronauts are said to change, is what I heard
After they have escaped from this world & then returned from space with their
Altered perceptions
Their flaming, falling star descent being infinitely more
Than a mere return to the patio
& bar-be-que in a Houston backyard
Where thick, vinelike St. Augustine grass
Cracks the driveway blacktop
Inside the silver skin of the fallen starship
Wilma Sue pulls Joe Harris down onto the fold-out bed
Wilma Sue licks the hairy chest of Joe Harris

Joe Harris longs to escape from the soft blue suede gravity of love forever
All Joe Harris was looking for was a big breakfast
Joe Harris longs for some country music to be playing
To dance his mind away to other dimensions, other times
To make his mind vanish like an electron into some secret orbit
Reading the restless, endlessly lonesome midnight movie mind of Joe Harris
Wilma Sue sez, You want to hear some radio?
Joe Harris had not even seen any radio in that room
Nor thought to tell Wilma Sue that if the truth be told
He was in reality an undercover radio repairman on vacation
To see if she would buy that
Some country music might be nice, sez Joe Harris
Come here then, sez Wilma Sue
Pulling Joe Harris down into the irresistible blue gravity
Into the perfect late night, color television tides
Of her heavenly body

The blue electric waves of its secret lagoons. Her skin as soft as blue suede
Blast off inside me, rocketboy, sez Wilma Sue in a whisper at his ear with her
Blue suede breath
& I'll see if I can dial us in some Patsy Cline
Sweet dreaming music to slowdance to
& commence some serious savior angel
Sweet sucking of necks, not to mention sundry
Body parts

GIANT NIGHT
(The Paranormal Poetry of Chaos Theory with Cameo by Steve McQueen and
Soundtrack Featuring Roy Orbison)
Recommended for Mature Audiences Only

Rainy sitting close to Joe Harris in the late night heat
The old Indian blanket seat cover itchy on his bare back
The sharp, ozone dampness of Rainy's body
As she leans with one arm hugging his shoulders & the stars
Arching above the interstate
Folding them in a sweet, secret skin of galactic light
Rainy leaning over to kiss Joe Harris
On his driving arm saying
I want to fuck you right out of your mind
Far out, sez Joe Harris
Rainy taking from her tiny, 1930s silver cigarette case
A fat joint of pure Colombian
On the radio Roy Orbison was warbling his old operatic ballad about lost love
In Dreams in an eerily high falsetto: A candy-colored clown they call the sandman
Tiptoes in my room. I just love this song, sez Rainy and begins singing
Along: Only in dreams, in beautiful dreams.
Let's stop near Peoria & get us a motel room, sez Rainy
& slowfuck this giant night away on the far out moons of Mars where there's no
Gravity and we can just float off into the giant night sky fucking
We're not waiting on me, sez Joe Harris, & puts the pedal to the metal
Who do you think you are anyhow, hoss, sez Rainy, with her blue velvet breath
Steve McQueen, the big movie star in some San Francisco chase scene?
I ain't no swinging dick, Steve McQueen macho man movie star, sez Joe Harris
Hey, hoss, sez Rainy, I just want you to be my candy-covered clown tonight
Don't you mean candy-colored? sez Joe Harris. Whatever you say, sez Rainy
Just as long as you tiptoe into my dreams tonight like some sandman with your
Stardust and swinging candy-covered dick
Do you believe in dreams, beautiful dreams?

EVEN THE STARS SOMETIMES MUST GET LONELY
(Poem with Pine Trees, Shotgun Blast, and Belt Buckle)

Under a cathedral stand of elegant pines, far from
The road, we spread a blanket half in shade &
Half in the sunlight, & Rainy untied her pale blue
Halter & leaned over me & kissed me very hard
I was trying to take off my shirt
No, Rainy said. Let me
Often Rainy would say this. Then she would
Unbutton your shirt & unbuckle your jeans &
Pull them off, & her hands & her lips would
Move all over your movie. It was very quick &
You could feel the warm rush of her movie gently
Moving your own movie into new spaces. But this was
Dangerous territory. I had been there. No maps
& Rainy might vanish, like any star at first dawn. But I always
Followed. I followed
Suddenly, from some distance there was a flat
Crisp sound, like gunfire. A shotgun maybe. Rainy
Looked up
It's nothing, I said
It's something, Rainy said. & she
Rolled away to the far edge of the blanket, & she
Lay with her back to me
Who had been approaching sleep
As though through a tunnel of trees
Under the falling leaves of the night
As the evening rose quietly up from the grass
The trees had been full of birds we could not see
Now they rose up into an evening cloud at the sound &
Floated away
We looked up & watched the dark fall upon them & us
Like a net of night
Harvesting stars like fish
The dark boat of our blanket
Drifted on water touched by warm wind
Our boat drifted over water
Fed by warm springs
Since childhood I had dreamed of Rainy's
Buried treasures waiting in the future for me alone
On some far shore
Marked by a foreign flag
Planted long before I was ever born

It's very far away, I said. Maybe five or
Ten miles. Please come back
Rainy said nothing. Her beautiful tan back
Curled into her shoulders. She held herself very tightly
I still felt light & high from her touch. But I
Could feel the energy reversing across the gaps
The electricities jumping backwards across orbits
Suddenly it was morning again
Time had failed for us
A body flooding back into the harsh canyon light
They couldn't reach us here, I said, trying to
Sound real
It's not the sound, Rainy said finally, still
Turned from me. I just got lost
I touched her back very gently. Rainy shivered
& pulled farther away
Lost, Rainy said
Lost, I tell you

SKULL MOVIES
(Poem with Dead Buffalo and Feathered Horns in a Dream Canyon Cinema)

I know what Rainy meant. It was happening
Again. I could tell, because there was no
Control. We were simply there. The landscape
Was much too clear, crisp, & white as bone
The skull of the buffalo
With feathered horns
The completed history
Of all buffaloes. Finished. Enclosed. Rainy
Curling into her fears: her body much too real
As if light projected through her, as if the
Dream itself shimmered into her. & when Rainy
Needs me I am gone into its vast emptiness, waiting
For a role. Brother, lover, friend, father
Sister. Any role, but soon
But all this has already happened
All of this was over. Dead as the Buffalo. Let
It go, I said to my secret self
But there were no words, no voice
No radio signal for me to capture from the airlike magic
Sometimes the
Trick is to flow close to Rainy's need, but not too
Close. It might be your own need
Rainy, I said, but I said nothing at all
All of this was over. Dead as the Buffalo. Let
It go, I said, but there were no words. All of
This has happened, I said to my secret self, but there was no
Voice. No radio
The trick is to feel the pain, but wear it
Like a movie mask. It might be your own. A role, a
Temporary shape, a skull for the light's passage
Into form. Into feathers. That was it. That was the trick
But no fakes. Not in this dream canyon
The sudden apparition of friends, or guardians
Join you in a circle. Hand in hand, a
Field, a circuit. A pure strong current of energy
They pass to you. Apparitions, the dead, a
Continuous connection, you see them here in bodies
Of your own imagining. So this is their secret
So this is their dream canyon. So this is it. Dead or
Alive. & you know how it will all go on without
You. Dead or alive. The choice. Choose. The
Trick is to treat the pain as your own. It is. It is

ONCE AGAIN

(Poem with Centuries of June Love, Planets, Electrons, Lovers, and Poems Safely in
Their Orbits)

It's OK, Rainy said. Rainy was kissing me
& she held me very tightly in her arms
It's all right, Rainy said. Rainy was no longer
At the edge of the blanket. Rainy was holding me
& rocking me just a little. The deep shade of
The pines covered us completely. I felt a small
Cool breeze across the pine needles, & it felt
Like evening falling, once again, forever

THE LIGHTS OUT THERE ON THE FREEWAY
(Poem with Sunflowers, Pipe, Pistol, Onions, Letter, and Bullet by Van Gogh)

When the dark came on, we went out
Through the screen door to the back porch
& we watched the lights flow over the bridge from Berkeley
Those lights are just the memory of energy, Joe Harris
Said
The sky was deep blue, except for the stars
Growing brighter, one by one
The Moon was a mere scary Moslem grin of absence
A light was on in
The room behind us, & the stereo, too
That Rainy McCall gal had come up from LA that very morning
Rainy, like her twin suicidal sister Pearl, was pretty much
Just another Hippie Princess from the lost age of Aquarius
Anyway, Rainy sat on the steps next to some sunflowers you could
Barely see in the electricity
Rainy brought out the homegrown weed from our fluorescent farm, our hydroponic
Paradise
We had grown it in magic water, with a special diet of
Chemicals, which were supposed to alter the
Genetic structure of the weed, & produce a
Higher quanta energy level
A quanta is a tiny bit of energy. We farmed relentlessly
For a quanta jump in the weed, when the electrons
Jump to a higher frequency orbit
Then, you smoke the orbit. New paths of
Motion appear
Anyway, so we farmed faithfully
Joe Harris, said Rainy, in her imitation
Of his slow country voice, whatever are you
Talking about, hoss?
The lights out there on the freeway, said Joe
Harris

(& speaking of sunflowers & yellow, said Charlie Trout, Gauguin stated: Colors are
their own meanings. Take Vincent van Gogh's sunflower paintings, still some of the
best still life around. He liked yellow & he worked with broad spreads of flat yellow
tones. Pretty amazing stuff. Then you look at his Still Life with Drawing Board &
it's something else entirely, a kind of self-portrait with items from his personal life
including his pipe, some onions, a prayer book, & a letter from his brother, plus
a pistol & one bullet, all laid out on his rough table, but without his own image
present.)

THE STAR OF THIS POEM
(Poem with Redwoods, Short Haircut, Kiss, and Famous Horse Named Trigger)

Jimmy, a Jamaican singer, sang on our
Stereo: he was a star, waiting for the tide
His voice, in its vinyl loop, sang
I'm sitting here in limbo-land
Waiting for the tide to come
That month, Charlie Trout had flown back from Jamaica
With the record, & with three pounds of ganji
A very religious weed grown there in the Voodoo Mountains
Charlie Trout intended to make a profit on the ganji, but
Found that he was so altered from smoking the
Ganji orbits, he was giving most of the ganji away
So far
Now, Charlie Trout was sitting on our porch, in the dark
& wonderful redwoods, seventy miles north of
SeaCity, singing a little harmony with the stereo
Joe Harris, Joe Harris, said Rainy, express yourself
Boy. Charlie Trout laughed, & I did too
Rainy had her hair cut very short by then
To look like a flapper girl, she said
& she moved her
Fingers through it now. Rainy always seemed to
Like to caress herself
I snapped off a sunflower & leaned over to place it
Behind Rainy's ear. Now, said I to Rainy, if you had not cut off all your long black hair
You could wear that flower like your very own halo
Yellow is my very favorite color, said Rainy McCall
Yellow is the pure color of electricity, said Charlie Trout
Joe Harris leaned his chair back, to look up
At the stars. Joe Harris
Had very long cowboy bones
It takes many human lifetimes for that there starlight to reach
Our human eyes, said Joe Harris. So what we see is a movie
Projected from the past. Like a memory
When Joe Harris talked like this, we liked
To get on his case. Joe Harris was from Oklahoma, &
He liked to talk like this
Charlie Trout passed me a joint of the Jamaican
He pressed his index finger very softly against
My own, until I held the smoke
Inhaling, I moved into a loop: the Voodoo Mountains
Of Jamaica, vinyl memory, the stars & the lights on the bridge
Then, the record ended
Are you the star of this here poem, Joe Harris?
Asked Rainy in her imitation country voice

Joe Harris went & put his arm around Rainy
Joe Harris held Rainy, & he did not say anything
For a long, long time
Any old time you see me, sweetheart, said Joe Harris at last
Rainy laughed & kissed Joe Harris hard, & we
All clapped our hands, & hooted, just like at
The end of an old Western Movie when
The hero gets hisself kissed
By his faithful & famous horse Trigger. Or is it vice versa?

A THIMBLE THEATER FOR BABY PLANETS IN THEIR BABY ORBITS
(Poem with Backyard, Breakfast, Sleeping Bag, Drive-In Movie, Blue Halter Top, Old Black Ford, and Ruins of Babylon)

In the morning Rainy & Joe Harris
Cooked up a big old breakfast & put it
On a bare pine door, which was the kitchen
Table. We had some tea, & then biscuits
With honey, & then fried eggs with Portuguese
Sausages, & then sweet sliced tomatoes
After this, Rainy & I went out to the
Backyard, to catch some rays
I suspect Rainy slept with Joe Harris. She has already slept with Charlie Trout
I suspect
I slept with a sleeping bag. Some sleep!
Like a transistor radio, a '55 Ford was
Giving us the business in the corner of the
Movie
It was a Black Ford, rusting out on
The blocks next to the garage. Some Ford!
Remember when Pearl came up from Berkeley
& we smoked those really skinny numbers?
Rainy asked me
Sure, I said in my sure voice
It was the night we made love in the Ford
It was the first time
The grasses were up to the rear windows
The backseat was like a drive-in movie. The images
Of your body kept on changing. Some dope! It was just like
That time on the blanket under that cathedral of pines when our boat
Drifted into the dimension
Of another world entirely & you became lost to me
In this world
It was going to be a hot one all right
Tiny circles of sweat glittered on Rainy's
Pretty tan arms. In the corner of the windshield
Of the Ford, across the yard of sun & mist, a
Tiny American flag decal waved old glory
I feel silly talking about the past, I said
You don't have to say anything, Rainy said
But I wanted to tell her about the drive-in movie
Part. Every time I sat & looked at the Black Ford
I remembered those shifting takes. Rainy, sweet Rainy
Not Rainy, not, Rainy again. Some drive-in movie part!
I don't know how to say this, I said
What's that, sweetheart? Rainy said

That night, I said. I kept losing your body
First you were there, & then you were not
That's easy, Rainy said, & pulled her blue halter
Up just a little bit. Huh? I said I wasn't there all the time, Rainy said
Where were you? I said
It was going to be a hot one all right. A
California Blue Jay appeared, for a cool drink
From the pan on the stump
I was in the 10th century, Rainy said. I
Was a small boy in a village, in Persia, near ruins of the ancient city of
Babylon

WARM RADIO
(Poem with Blue Donkey Beads, Mosque, California Blue Jay, Contraceptive Foam,
and Message Written in Blue Stones for the Ages)

When I sit & look at the Ford, I
Do not want to think of SeaCity, but
SeaCity is there, like a ruin, or a radio
Signal
If you do not need the signal, I surely
Understand
But the radio of the Black Ford did not
Ask any questions. SeaCity transmitted the
Signal, the radio received it, & sent it
Out again, clearly, unless you turned the
Dial wrong, or your tubes burned out
Later, there was no battery. But the
Signal from SeaCity was still in the air
On clear days, Rainy said, we went to
A great city called Isfahan, to market. My
Father made bronze donkey beads, & we hung
Them with bells on the neck of our donkey
Rainy watched the California Blue Jay
Drink from the pan of cool water. I watched
Rainy's beautiful lips move, & I wondered &
Wondered
Vanish, said the radio of the Black Ford
that first time with Rainy. But it was
Only a commercial for a contraceptive foam
I turned the dial. Rainy kissed me
There was a mosque in Isfahan, Rainy
Said, with a message written in blue stones above
Its arched entrance, which said REALITY IS THE SHIFTING FACE OF NEED
AS WE BECOME WHO WE IMAGINE WE ARE

YOU MIGHT WONDER
(Poem with Blankets from Babylon, Guitar, Scraps of Velvet and Denim, Seven
Armed Robberies, and Beautiful Seashells on a Moonlit Beach)

You might wonder, Who is this Rainy McCall chick?
& who is Joe Harris? & who is this Charlie Trout character? & who are "we"?
It is a very good question
We wonder ourselves
We all wandered vaguely West across America
To crash those Golden Gates into
The Age of Aquarius with flowers
In our hair
Now, Rainy is a beautiful young woman
She has sun-browned, lovely skin
The approximate color of yellow roses as you have been told
Yes, please imagine if you will yellow roses in moonlight
Imagine the tropical light of colored television
Flowing like moonlight over
Avenues of yellow roses
You may wonder about the scent of Rainy's lovely, brown skin
After she has made love on a hot afternoon in August
So, once again, if you would please indulge me, folks
Imagine the smell of yellow roses
In a warm summer rain
Imagine the crushed rose scent of Rainy's underarms
Imagine the scent of Rainy's damp inner thighs
Those special, secret, tropical Edens of original scents
Where I have confessed we all lived to lick
Rainy has long
Graceful legs. Rainy makes her own
Clothes, from beautiful scraps of velvet
& denim. Rainy makes love with an astonishing
Abandon. Rainy tells you amazing facts
About the universe & her own needs. Rainy has small breasts
Which are wonderfully firm, & delicious
To kiss
Rainy plucks her guitar & sings Patsy Cline songs
Like the ghost of Janis Joplin
If you dare to look into Rainy's green eyes for
A long, long time, what you will see is
The mystery of memory

& Joe Harris, he is a handsome man
From Tulsa who wears a cowboy hat over his
Long blonde, hippie hair, & Joe Harris drives a
Well-tuned Ford pickup truck with a magic camper
Room in the back, where you rest on blankets Joe Harris claims are
From Babylon, & you see the morning rise
In the light drifting through a stained-glass
Window he installed himself. Joe Harris is as good a carpenter as Jesus, &
A funky guitar picker, & a very slow & kind lover
Rainy tells me to make me cry. If you look & look into
The mild blue eyes of Joe Harris, you will see
Many, many secrets
Of the Old West
One thing I do know for sure
& Charlie Trout, he is a big hillbilly from West Virginia, who can be very scary
Sometimes. Charlie Trout pulled seven armed robberies the summer he was
Seventeen (four cabs & three bars in Atlantic City, New Jersey) after he had run
Away from his home in the hills. He tries to act like a grade-B movie gangster, but
Basically he has the mild personality of a trout, mostly bemused and beguiled easily
He protects us when we travel out into the faraway foggy neighborhoods on the
Electric trolleys for dope deals in the thuggy bars. He saves our secrets and mysteries
In poems he collects like lovely seashells on a moonlit beach
One thing I do know for sure
Their voices. Their voices are as true blue as the songs
Of Mockingbirds coming
Over our old radio

DOUBLE TAKES
(Poems About Ordinary Things Observed in the Mysterious Rearview Mirrors of
Poetry as They Vanish into the Past, Mirrors in Which Objects May Appear to Be
Closer than They Actually Are)

a.
Poem with Wings

As the windows flare & darken & flare
A little cloud & its shadow float
North across an airport parking lot
Into a winter field
If you could
Just get yourself together
The white exhaust idles over a new snow
So far from the old love poems of the past

You can move anywhere now, alone
Just now you follow the little cloud
Toward a single leafless tree
& beneath it, like a fist
Relaxing, a fire in a barrel
Above its branches a flight rises smaller
& smaller. Is this Rainy vanishing again
A soft ash drifting
Into the pale yellow of the sun?
Do you miss her? Will you
Touch yourself?
The stalks lean with an answer & quiver
The field brightens
With their luminous seeds
Which scatter in their thousand directions
You turn back to the lot
The flurries are lost
In themselves. The violet road burns
At its edge. You are near dark
On the interstate
Driving away from
An empty house called home alone
In the hills ahead, red taillights
Drift in a curve
Becoming one
Soon you will pass them, fragile & transparent
As the wings of your poem
Into the future
Wings of snow flurries
Fluttering in headlights
& frozen breath

b.
Poem Full of Past

The poem full of past has grown extreme like a baggie with too many memories of
Rainy
Floating around in it

If you look into it you might think of a flooded road
Rolling through a landscape you can almost recall
As though from a ruined dream
Of rapidly approaching headlights
With an old stone church beside the road & an overgrown, collapsed graveyard
Nearby, & blackbirds drifting low as though over
A smashed body
You might think of the thin hard needles of steel beneath the dream
To hold it up
When the dream cracks open, you can see them
Mostly in spring this happens
When the world warms
If you look at the poem in sunlight you may think of a church window
Or the narrow stained-glass neck of a blackbird swallowing a brightly banded snake
The light glowing through the thin
Membranes making a rainbow as the poem expands
The memories may appear to grow smaller through the
Membranes. Don't believe it. It may be that you aren't
Watching closely enough. Concentrate
Like the hedges. Can you honestly say you see some spring buds?
Don't touch those buds or they will die
If you are tired of the poem or are hungry
Please do not press through the poem, please
You may only look
If you do press through the poem
Even with a soft part
Of your body, your nipple or palm
Or penis
The memories may melt
Like old hopes & dreams left
Out overnight in rain & snow

16
LOVE AT THE EDGE OF THE GALAXY
(Poem with Movie, Corner Lot, and Orgasm)

In the corner lot
Returning from the old movies
In the backseat of the old broke down Black Ford
Rainy & I found
The orgasm completely

17
DO YOU BELIEVE YOUR DREAMS ARE REAL?
(Poem with Blue Velvet Robe, Palm Trees, Snow in Los Angeles, Beautiful Breasts, and Masturbation)

Do you believe your dreams are real? Rainy asked. It was February
Early morning in her bedroom back in LA. We agreed it was another fantasy
We wouldn't make it. But here I was again
Believe them? I asked. How do you mean believe?
She lay quietly for a moment. You could see the pale glow
Of her small, beautiful breasts in the light which filtered in through
The morning coastal fog & the hazy yellowing breath of the nearby
Freeway
You know, Rainy said. Do you think they are real?
I don't know exactly what you mean, I said, though I thought
I might know all too well. My own reality edges were blurring
Too: a soft, out-of-focus coast of dream & morning freeway, rusting
Chrome on the Ford's dark surface, lush flowers & palms at the rushing
Edge, lost in the windshield's reflection of speed, metal
& chemical air
Well, Rainy said, listen & then tell me: We were
Living back East, in two tall apartment buildings which faced each
Other across an alley. You looked at me through your window. I
Looked at you through mine. My window was open, & it snowed in a
Little, & I wore my blue velvet robe. You remember the one? I
Unbuttoned it, & dropped it to the floor, to show you my body, &
To touch myself. You know what I mean. The snow came in the window
& melted on my body. You motioned to me to come over. But I
Wanted, instead, to touch myself & you to watch. & I looked
Down onto the alley & there was a girl you know, one I had seen you
With many times. I called & waved to her. She laughed when she
Saw I had no clothes on, & she waved back. Then, suddenly, I saw
Her in your apartment. You were both laughing & she kissed you
& you began to make love, I could see it all. It was very exciting watching you
& the snow melting as it hit my
Hot skin

THAT GIRL YOU WERE MAKING LOVE TO LAST NIGHT IN SOME SLEAZY
MOVIE OF MY LIFE
(Poem with Fresh Oranges, Old Japanese Grocer, and Color Television Set)

When I left Rainy that morning I could not erase the image of
Snow melting on her bare body
Well, one thing I do know for sure. It never really snowed
In LA that February. Unless you count the snow you could rarely
See in the high mountains which rim the hazy bowl of the big LA
Basin. Or the snow of late night, color teevee
I stopped in a small Japanese supermarket to buy some
Fresh oranges. & there it was: snow, falling across the polished
Aisles like flakes drifting down from the overhead fluorescents
All the gleaming cans, the boxes of Oriental noodles, the soft drinks
Flowed with its power. A small radio played over the frozen vegetable
Counter. I suddenly felt the interior of the market turn & spiral
Out in pure currents of electricity. Jesus, my secret self said
Get out of here. Buy an orange. Go back to the Ford. No
My secret self said, Flow
It is real, isn't it? Rainy asked. She was crying. I
Saw snow, like flakes of hazy light, falling across her lovely face

As she began to vanish again
No, I said, trying to sound real myself. That's only
A dream. You were so afraid to touch me then, she said, remember? I hadn't learned
How, I said. That's all over. Can't you remember last night?
The old Japanese grocer watched me turning into snow
He smiled & he said, Do you want to buy oranges to take back to the girl
This morning? & he laughed
& you know something else? Rainy asked. She turned
Toward me. Her eyes flashed, dazzling flatness
That dream girl, Rainy said, you were making love to last night
She looked just like me. Almost exactly like me. Like a double
In some sleazy movie of my life

AMAZING FINGERPRINTS
(Poem with Pool Game, Two Color Television Sets, and Happy Sheriff Show)

Up ahead, under the big dark redwoods
The pink neon circle glowed. The pink
Neon circle was the sign which invited you into
Tom's Timber Inn
Want to catch a quick cold one? asked
Joe Harris
Why not, answered I
Joe Harris slow-motioned his magic pickup
Into the dirt parking lot. Inside Tom hisself
Was tending bar. Tom hisself smiled, when he
Saw us enter. Two color teevees
Hovered at opposite ends of the bar
Right now, both color teevees were beaming
Hey, Tom, said Joe Harris. How come you got
Both tubes beaming?
Tom hisself smiled at Joe Harris
I don't want to miss anything, said Tom hisself
Some friends were shooting pool. Under
The circle of the pool light you could see
Charlie Trout, & Rainy gliding above the
Greenfelt surface, & sighting the holes very
Carefully
Charlie Trout put down his cue stick
Charlie Trout moseyed over to be friendly
Hey, buddy, said Charlie Trout to me, & reached
Out his hand for a shake
But when we shook our hands together, I saw
Something very very strange. The hand of Charlie
Trout was perfectly blue
Was this an Eye-Fantasy? No
Really, the hand of Charlie Trout was just
Covered with fine blue pool powder. You usually
Rub pool powder on the end of your cue stick
Charlie Trout had rubbed the fine blue
Pool powder all over his own hand
Hey, Charlie Trout, said I. What's with the blue hand?
Charlie Trout took a sip from the bottle of
Beer he held in his other, normal-colored hand
Too much all night color teevee, said Charlie Trout

I looked up at one of the color teevees
It was the Happy Sheriff Show. The Happy Sheriff
Was rocking on his front porch, watching a tiny
Portable color teevee. I looked back at Charlie Trout
Besides, said Charlie Trout, it leaves
Amazing fingerprints
That sure solves the mystery, then, said I to Charlie Trout
My old boyhood buddy, of where
The blue fingerprints
All over Rainy's beautiful breasts
Came from

THE LOVELY BOOK LEFT WITH THE DEAD FOR THEM TO READ
(Poem with Tropical Winter Room and Roller Derby as a Religious Way of Life)

Charlie Trout was not just a joker. In
The winter movies, Charlie Trout put down his cue stick
& said goodbye to Tom hisself & the Timber Inn
& goodbye to the two color teevees beaming across
Tom's Timber Inn
& then Charlie Trout followed the hard cold
Rains down the coast to SeaCity
There, Charlie Trout took his usual winter room
In the basement of an old Victorian mansion
His fluorescent farm
Tropical with hydroponic lights
There, Charlie Trout has a window over the backyard garden
Which slopes down to the bay & is covered with tangles
Of old rose bushes & honeysuckle vines
When you go to visit Charlie Trout in the
Winter movies, often he is working very hard
Watching his silent teevee. A silent teevee is
A teevee with no sound to be heard. You may wonder how
This is work
It is a good question
For, you see, Charlie Trout is a foreign
Correspondent for the SeaCity All-Star Savior Angels
The toughest & most fierce of all female roller derby
Teams. Charlie Trout's main job is to write dispatches
Praising the valor & bravery & beauty of the fierce females
Of the SeaCity All-Star Savior Angels as they spin
& glide & attack the electric forms
Of other brave, gliding fierce females in the
Screenspace universe of Charlie Trout's silent teevee
So far, however, the SeaCity All-Star Savior Angels have never
Met a foreign team from, say, Mars
So, says Charlie Trout, I am a foreign
Correspondent limited to the planet Earth
Also, when Charlie Trout is not watching his silent
Teevee, or simply sipping a cold beer, Charlie Trout
Works on his never-to-be-finished Great American Novel, known
Some days as The Lovely Book Left with
The Dead for Them to Read, or
Other days as The Romances and Mysteries of
Rainy McCall

21
FAVORITE ANCESTOR
(Poem with Sunlight from Garden of Ancient Roses and Honeysuckle, Full-Blood
Hopi Indian, Old Western Movie, and Soap Opera Stars Shining Brightly in the
Afternoon)

Joe Harris & me & Charlie Trout
Spent a warm lazy afternoon in Charlie
Trout's big winter tropical room, lazing about in the bright
Sunlight from the garden, while watching
Old black & white Western Movies on the Silent teevee, & talking about the past
Who is your favorite ancestor? I asked
Joe Harris
Oh, said Joe Harris, stretching his long
Cowboy bones, I reckon that would be Grandma Harris
She was a full-blood Hopi Indian. That old woman, she
Knew some amazing secrets about the Old West
I looked at the long blonde cowboy hair of Joe Harris
Shining in the light from the garden of ancient yellow roses &
Honeysuckle. I looked into the mild blue cowboy eyes
Of Joe Harris
Well then, Joe Harris, said I. Where do you get
Them blue cowboy eyes & that wig of blonde cowboy hair?
The crow's feet in the corners of the mild blue
Eyes of Joe Harris crinkled up into a smile
That there is one of the old Indian's best kept secrets
An old Western Movie glowed on Charlie Trout's
Silent teevee. You could barely see the old Western
Movie amid the bright light from the garden of ancient roses
& honeysuckle like the neon
Of a motel in the bright, early morning, blinking
Vacancies as pale as the ghost
Of the redskin brave who bit the dust in the old Western Movie. A cowboy hero killer
Rode off into the sunset
Toward Dream Canyon
You got any favorites in your family tree?
I asked Charlie Trout about his own ancestors
The old Western Movie turned to snow. Charlie
Trout reached out to switch the channel to
Rainy's very favorite soap opera: As Galaxies Collide
Sure, said Charlie Trout. The afternoon
Teevee stars
In tragic soap operas about
Seduction & the betrayal of best
boyhood friends & faithless
Lovers with short, black, shiny
Flapper girl haircuts

69

SECRET SHELL
(Poem with Shore of Ancient Forgotten Sea, the American Midwest, and Pedestrians)

As you might now suspect, sitting in
Charlie Trout's big winter tropical room is a real
Mystery trip. Yellow sunshine
Flowing from the ancient hillside garden, & pale
Streams of winter television light
Only The Shadow Knows, that old
Mystery show playing low
On the old pink Silvertone radio in the corner on a chair
Like a murmur from some secret lost shore shell
From the bottom of a forgotten sea
Never a straight wave to be had
Sitting in this secret shell was like finding
Your movie in some strange, vast Intersection in
The Middle West, with traffic flowing in from
The distant vanishing points, & the light
Changes, & as you step into the street, you
No longer see pedestrians separately, or traffic, but
Rather you feel the flow of their movements
Together in a fine clear frequency
You know what I like about frequencies
Charlie Trout sez, is that they is frequent
Like fucking flapper girls a
Whole lot
On hot August afternoons

WHEN ELECTRONS JUMP ORBITS
(Poem with Marshmallows and Peyote)

When electrons jump orbits, they disappear for a spell, said Joe Harris
As the winter rain continued to pelt
The winter window panes
Rainy & Joe Harris & me & Charlie Trout were inside toasting
Marshmallows in the color teevee, making
Plans for our exit to SeaCity
Where do they go? Rainy wanted to know, &
Leaned out to make a delicate adjustment
On the magenta dial of the color teevee
The long blonde cowboy hair of Joe Harris
Changed hue slightly
Nobody seems to remember, said Joe Harris
They become ghosts of electricity, said Charlie Trout, & then Charlie Trout said to
Rainy
Would you please stop fucking around with that teevee dial, please
Like you are playing with a dick or something?

24

THE RADIANCE OF A STAR
(Poem with Boy from Babylon, Old Ford, Tarzan, and Salt)

a

I looked again at the rusting axles
Of the old Black Ford & I wondered what had become
Of the wheels
Rainy put an arm around my waist &
Rested her head very lightly on my shoulder
Which was shaped like a baby bear
Do you think I am crazy? Rainy asked me
I smelled the clean dampness of her body
No, I heard my voice say from some vast
Distance. & I saw myself lean & kiss sweet
Rainy
Later, I decided this: That giant night in
The old Black Ford, Rainy had just left her
Bodyspace, at times, for a moviespace
& moviespaces do not ask any questions
Moviespaces receive the signals, & they
Show the movies
So, you might say that Rainy was more a star beamed from deep space
Than a real Persian boy living
In another century or dimension near
The ancient ruins of Babylon
I, myself, have never completely understood
The source, or space, or time of moviespaces
Yet I love to be, however briefly, near
The radiance of a star
Still, this I must confess: Sadly, I learned
Always to take my stars with a grain
Of salt

Tarzan's former costar & movie son, Johnny Sheffield
Who played the role of Boy, said of Tarzan
I can only say that working with Tarzan was one of the highlights of my life
He was a Star (with a capital "S"), & he gave off a special Radiant light
& some of that light got into me
Knowing & being with Tarzan during my formative years
& messing around like a monkey with a near naked Maureen
O'Sullivan in utter simian abandon on a set
Designed to look like the dark heart
Of an African jungle
With a secret graveyard piled with the bleached bones &
Abandoned ivory of ancient herds of ancestor elephants
Had a lasting influence
On my life

Star Light, Star Bright
First Star I see this giant night
I wish I may
I wish I might
Have the wish I
Make tonight
To live like a Persian boy ripe with radiance
& grace
Near the ruins of old
Babylon
Before I finally rise to become a star
In my own right
Alone in the sunrise
El Hombre, ancient & foreign
By nightfall

THE TRAGIC DEATH OF TELEVISION
(Tropical Poem with Fedora and Naked Trout)

As always, Charlie Trout floated
In his big white tub in the corner of his
Winter room, sipping a cool beer
& watching old black & white movie classics on his silent teevee through the warm
& comfortable waves of rising steam
Sitting there grinning, his old battered
Gangster fedora pulled low over his fishy eyes
Malo malo, said Charlie Trout, as we walked
Into the tropical winter room
Hi, Charlie Trout, said I. What's with the
Mumbo jumbo?
Nada nada, said Charlie Trout. I am
Practicing on my chants, that's all. Look at here
Charlie Trout pointed with his beer bottle
At the steamy mirror above his big white tub
Sure enough there was a chant, written in ghostlike dew
As we become what we imagine we are
Read the chant
Mama rama, said Charlie Trout. I better get
Out of this pond & get ready
Ready for what, Charlie Trout? asked I
Charlie Trout slid out of his big white tub, into
The bright sunlight from the garden
His big body naked & glistening
His silvery scales shining like
Neon rainbows on a rainy midnight street in the tropics
I had to wonder if Rainy McCall had seen his big naked trout body
In all the glory of its glistening scales
The tragic death of television, said Charlie Trout
& clicked off the silently playing
Teevee in the corner of the tropical
Winter room
& rerun resurrection in the waves
Far downstream in the flow
Said Charlie Trout as he clicked the
Magic machine on once
Again. Adios, hello again
Said Charlie Trout. & goodbye
At the end of love, Amen

MYSTERY MUSIC
(Poem with Blue Cowboy Eyes, Fogbound Beach, and Infinite Sadness)

Joe Harris looked over, with mild
Surprise in his blue cowboy eyes
OK, Charlie Trout, said Joe Harris. What's the big
Secret?
No secret, said Charlie Trout. I joined the
Buddha Buddies, & I am practicing my
Chants, & my new Buddha Buddy, George
He is coming by directly to chant
Holy Moses, said Joe Harris. Them Zen hoods
They'd steal anything not nailed down
You best hide your radio
I looked over at Charlie Trout's old pink
Silvertone radio, like a mystery shell from a forgotten
Ocean. I looked back at Joe Harris's blue
Cowboy eyes & I grinned
I went over to Charlie Trout's old pink
Silvertone mystery shell. I clicked it on. There was
An old mystery show playing, with old mystery
Music
Only The Shadow Knows was
The old mystery show on the ancient
Silvertone mystery shell
Next to the Silvertone mystery shell, there was an empty
Amber tinted Tennessee whiskey bottle, with a sprig of
Dried honeysuckle. Charlie Trout came over to the ancient Silvertone
Mystery shell, & with both his mystery fins on the
Dials, Charlie Trout tuned in the mystery
Music very very clearly
Music full of infinite sadness & longing
Like the muffled sounds of unseen surf
Ghost waves breaking on a fogbound beach
Of some lost ghost shore
Of an inland ocean long
Buried beneath mountains with snow
On their peaks, or maybe more
Like an oldie but goodie sung by Rainy
McCall from the distant future
Oh, said Charlie Trout. My radio is always hidden
& Rainy McCall ain't coming over today, so don't hold your
Breath, boys

THE MYSTERIOUS ART OF MIGRATION
(Poem with Salt Marshes, Pickup Truck, Dinosaur Bones and Blood, and Rainy McCall Nowhere in Sight)

We zoomed on, over the Crystal
Creek Bridge, about as far from Rainy McCall as we all could get that day, & then we
Were
Spinning along the Bay & the
Shimmering salt marshes
In our windshieldspace, on the bright
Shallows, a tall white bird slept
On one pink leg
Not many of them birds left, said
Joe Harris
Nope, said Charlie Trout. Beautiful mommas
Ain't they?
The engine of Joe Harris's magic pickup
Was so finally tuned you could not hear it
Work. It did not seem true that the engine
Was burning ancient dinosaur bones &
Blood, just a short distance below
Our feet. In fact, it seemed
The engine was a silent container
A perfectly designed shape
Which did not burn blood & bones at all
But rather merely gathered
& channeled some ghost energies
You could not see, or smell, or
Touch. That there Joe Harris
He was nobody's fool when it came
To motion. Quicker
Than a wink, we landed
On the coast. For such a hot
Day, there was almost no one
There. We hoofed it nearly a mile down the dazzling
White sand. There were rows & rows
Of long bluegreen waves flopping
In from China
On wings of water
We passed piles of shells
Pink & nearly transparent
& orange & purple shells
& even shells black as the toenails of trolls

We passed the body of a half buried
Dead seagull. The feathers of the
Dead seagull ruffled out into the light
& in the breeze, one
Wing pointed south
Toward SeaCity, the lost kingdom
Of Rainy McCall
You know something, said Charlie
You could make about a million lenses
Out of all this here white sand
To help see stars lost
To the naked eye

When Marilyn Monroe was discovered
Dead, naked, & facedown
On her bed, an empty fifty-pill bottle of
Nembutals near her blazing lamp
The effect on LA's Skid Row was chaotic
The transients & bums in that city
Of lost angels & light & projection talked
Of little else, & many began
To move
It is such events that may trigger a primal need to migrate
Relying on irrational rumors
That life is better or safer
Someplace else

THE TRUTH FOSSILS TELL YOU
(Poem with White Wine, Fairies, and Waves Flopping in from China like
Wings of Water)

When we reached Driftwood Point
We sat for a spell in a small
Circle, & we got out the jug
Of white wine, & the numbers
The Middle West was once an ocean
Said Joe Harris. Joe Harris should
Know. Joe Harris was born in Tulsa
The shit you say? said Charlie Trout
You bet, said Joe Harris. If you can
Believe fossils
The truth fossils tell you
Listen to this one here, Joe Harris
Said & held a smooth white shell
Up to his ear & grinned
You want to listen real close
To what your fossils want to say to you
About the future
Which sounds very much like Niagara Falls
Or Rainy's laughter after love
In the afternoon.
Holy moly, Joe Harris, said I. That there
Shell is shaped like a strange slipper
Like the strange slipper of some little fairy
You mean, said Charlie Trout, eyeballing
Me from beneath the low brim
Of his battered gangster fedora
One of them homosexual human being
Types? No, said I. I mean
One of them funny little magical folks
Who run around over there in lands
Like Ireland, leprechauns & such
Who might have lived in the ghost
Forests around them lost oceans
Joe Harris was telling about
Far fucking out, said Joe Harris
You know something, said Charlie Trout
You could make a million lenses
Out of all this here white sand
To help see stars dark
To the naked eye

Far fucking out, said Joe Harris
Then Charlie Trout handed me
A smoking number
I took a puff
The tall bluegreen waves slowed
Like a surf of freezeframes
As they flopped in
Slower & slower
From China
I put the smooth, white shell
Shaped like the fossil
Of some ancient fairy's strange slipper
On my bare foot
It fit fine as wine

THE DAY ELECTRICITY QUIT COLD
(Poem Set in Wichita Falls, Texas, with Man in Barrel, Air Conditioning,
Cottonwoods, and Coming Storm)

All I know about Niagara Falls is from a movie newsreel
I saw as a boy in Wichita Falls, Texas. My big brother
& I paid one dime each to leave the 105-degree big Texas heat
& enter the air conditioned Linda Theater that whispered
To us inside like giant cottonwoods along
A river branch. In the bright window of the screen
A man was going to shoot over Niagara Falls in a barrel
I asked my big brother why
To de-fy Death, my big brother told me
To prove that he is a real man
In all the years I lived in Wichita Falls, Texas
I never got to see the falls there. When I asked
My big brother where the falls were he said
They are gone. The Indians took them
With their teepees when they left this land
The man in the barrel never got to de-fy death
Or prove he was a real man. Niagara Falls
Crashed & spilled out toward us
Like huge clouds of stardust
The man in the barrel, a tiny dark speck at the top
Of the screen, began his descent. Suddenly
The film stopped cold. It was my first
Freezeframe. It was my first
Broken narrative. We leaned forward
In our seats, breathless, suspended in the cool
Timeless darkness. Then the light of the window
Itself faded & the music of the soundtrack murmured
To a dead silence. All I could hear was the cool
Rush of the air conditioning like big cottonwoods
In a coming storm. It don't matter anyhow
My big brother said, as we walked along
The shining railroad tracks toward home. It was his movie double anyhow
His movie double? I asked my big brother. What's that anyhow?
Every star has a double, my big brother told me. That way
The stars never get killed so they can be in their next
Movie. Stars' movie doubles look just exactly like
The stars do & they do all the dangerous
Stunts for the stars. Like going over
Niagara Falls in a barrel
Well, what happened to the movie itself? Didn't
The movie itself have a movie double? I
Asked my big brother as we walked home in the big Texas heat

The electricity just quit cold on us, is what my big brother told me about that
& you know something else, Rainy would ask me many years later in my life
As she turned toward me, her eyes flashing, dazzling flatness
That girl, Rainy would say in her early morning bedroom in LA
A lifetime later, you were making love to last night
She looked exactly like me. Almost exactly like me. Like
A double in some sleazy movie
Of my life

LUNCH HOUR ON A FORBIDDEN PLANET NAMED LOVE
(Poem with Suggestion of Oral Sex)

It is time again
It is my lunch hour so I go
I walk down by the dark river
I want to be sure to reach Rainy in time
Rainy approaches me carrying a book
Rainy is bright, tremendous, wow
Rainy will like their green upstairs bedroom I hope
Honeybees between our bare toes crawl & tickle
We are nude beneath our costumes
We are looking for someplace good to eat
I desire your member in my mouth, sez that Rainy McCall gal
Groovy, sez I
Let us practice 69, sez Rainy
Far out, sez I
We orbit about one another
Like binary stars spinning
In the giant night sky of love
After our moveable feast I walk
Rainy back to her bookstore
Along the way I punch out this pirate of love
Who winks at Rainy
Who is my love all alone
In this little poem at least

THE FINAL INTERSTELLAR SKULL
(Poem with Phone Booth, Electric Trolley, Candlestick Park, Giant's Game, and One
Apple)

This phone booth faces the edge of America
46th Avenue, San Francisco, at the sandy end
Of the Judah Street electric trolley line. Within
The aluminum frame of its west wall, through
Double-thick safety glass, Joe Harris can see
The giant Pacific Ocean, vanishing
In sunset. Giant greygreen waves flare & fade
As a giant bank of evening fog approaches, cutting
The remaining light like film through a
Projector. The west wall itself glows pink
& nearly transparent. It is the Perfect
Booth
In the frame of the north wall of this Perfect
Booth, Joe Harris can see the great sheer cliffs
Of Marin County vanish in the cold fog
Joe Harris doesn't want to go out again
Into the cold wind whipping down 46th Avenue
Joe Harris fiddles with the coin return, spins
The dial aimlessly. DIALING LONG DISTANCE
IS THE NEXT BEST THING TO BEING
THERE a sign above the phone
Reminds Joe Harris. An electric trolley
Appears in the frame, wheeling slowly
& certainly around the turnabout here
At the end of the line. 46th Avenue &
There are no remaining passengers. The
Lights within its shining secret shell flicker briefly
As the cable clicks around the turn
& sends blue electric sparks into the fog
The driver, a big black dude, with a Van Dyke
Beard, wears cool shades. He reaches forward
In his seat to touch something. Maybe to dial
His transistor radio to a sunny Candlestick
Park Giants' game. Most of all
Joe Harris would like to dial Rainy
Long distance, Rainy, old-time lover
Lost somewhere along
The rural highways of rerun America

Maybe in a smoky, kerosene lit cabin
In the Northern Rockies, maybe in the electric
Pool of a clean, well lighted valley motel
Somewhere maybe in the pale, bluegreen mercury
Vapor lakes of the Midwest, or somewhere on the coast
In LA, maybe, city of light & projection
Joe Harris spins the dial of the phone aimlessly
Waiting for a dial tone. His dialing finger is very tan
From weeks on the coast. The rosy light filling
The Perfect Booth darkens his hair &
Features, giving the reflection of Joe Harris's face
In the glass door of the Perfect Booth
A smooth flat look, like the face of a dead Indian
Printed from an old negative. Do you think
We could try this again? Rainy
Had asked Joe Harris, after months
Back at the farm, of smoking this one plant
Taking Joe Harris past edges he had never known
Existed: the blueblack, insectlike sheen
Of light at the edge of the road up
To the old apple orchard where the remaining
Four trees had that last year yielded one apple
The sudden, glaring aluminumlike eye
Of the once friendly black & white
Teevee. The dazzling flatness of Rainy's eyes
The edges of her body shifting away across
The vastness of the big double bed. Image
& flesh blending, projecting across the curve
The timeless dome, the bone white
Screen. Rainy's voice, carrying across the oldest
Long distance in the universe to reach
Here, in the Perfect Booth
Here, at the end of the line, the
Final interstellar skull

PRETTY HIPPIE CHICK
(Poem with Joint, Mexican Sandals, Cadillac Cowboy, Invisible Door, Sleeping Child,
and Giant Night)

In the pink west wall of this Perfect Booth
The giant disk of the sun is descending into the waves
Joe Harris decides to smoke a number before
Trying to con a free ride from the black dude driver
On the electric trolley car at the end of the line. Joe Harris
Lights the number, good Colombian
Inhales deeply & blows smoke out
Toward the south wall where the evening
Neon of the Cliffs Motor Inn glows orange
Through the fog. Joe Harris watches his face
Reflected in the south wall of the Perfect Booth
Smiles & mugs a few poses, shaping
Ghosty identities for the coming evening
Hip young street dude hanging out
Cadillac cowboy with temporary engine trouble
Cool cardplayer looking for real action, endless
Frames, fossils of all sorts of futures. Just
As Joe Harris sees his movie shift again, a pretty hippie
Chick in a long, pale green & red flowered
Dress, Mexican
Sandals, appears in the frame of the west
Wall. She smiles through the invisible
Door between them, makes a pantomime knock
Joe Harris swings the invisible door wide open, smoke
From the half smoked number flowing out into the chilly early
Evening air. Could I use the poem for
A second? asks the pretty hippie chick
Sure thing, Joe Harris hears himself say in
A friend showing up with wine & good dope
Just before dinner voice. I'm just killing time
Waiting for the trolley to turn around here
At the end of the line
From the nearby passenger shelter, Joe Harris watches
The pretty hippie chick spin the dial effortlessly
Joe Harris wonders about who is the lucky connection
The pretty hippie chick's hair is black, like Rainy's
Long though, much longer, & Joe Harris notices
Suddenly what he thought was a pack on her back
Is not a backpack at all. It is a sleeping
Child, its head resting against her long black hair
Its tiny face like a movie double
For his own

The pretty hippie chick holds the poem
Gracefully as if it were the hand of
A loved one. Whereupon the pretty hippie chick replaces
The poem carefully in its cradle, opens
The invisible door & strolls slowly over
Toward Joe Harris, smiling as though Joe Harris
Is somebody she has missed for a very long time
You can have your interstellar skull back now, the pretty hippie chick
Says to Joe Harris & she winks like a sassy savior angel
As she sashays off toward the shining secret shell
Of the waiting electric trolley car ride to wherever
She needs to travel to in the giant night

MOTEL SOAP
(Poem with Empty Bed, Gideon Bible, Gothic Wife, Pool Shaped like a Human
Kidney, and Rip Tide)

The hardest part would be the long nights
With only the continuous flash & rush
Of headlights across the room's ceiling for company
Neon washing across the clean sheets of the big
Empty bed you couldn't sleep in. & strangely
The worst was in the mornings, your hands
Did not smell of Rainy's body. Your hands & beard smelled
Like motel soap. Ivory? Dial? Lifebuoy, maybe,
But you knew to stay with Rainy in that motel
In the Midwest, any longer would have been
Simple & pure madness. At least
The motel room had the appearance of
Sanity. At least that. The blue
Towels. The water glass in the translucent
Glassine wrapper. The Gideon
Bible. The color teevee, thank you, Jesus
The pastel postcards picturing the motel
Manager, his gothic wife, plus two beefy
Babes with shellpink blubber lounging
Safely by a pool shaped like the kidney
Of a human being. Forgetting a girl
Like Rainy
Was about as easy as forgetting you
Were drowning in a rip tide
In the middle of the summer vacation
At Virginia Beach your parents had taken you on
In honor of your high school graduation
The greatest achievement of your whole life
Up to that point in
The poem of your
Life

A DAY OFF FOR THE DEAD
(Poem with Kentucky Fried Chicken, Budweiser Beer, and Good Weather)

It was my day off & I had just had
Some Kentucky Fried Chicken & a can
Of Budweiser
So I felt like a million bucks
I would have gotten bombed that afternoon
But I had done that the day before
I had been thinking a lot
About Rainy again
I wish I could have just called her up
Out of the blue
Rainy kidded that it was colder than a witch's tit
Back there
I just wish I could have rubbed it
In a little that it was
Shirt sleeve weather where I was
I might have headed on over
To Santa Monica
For a walk on the beach
I wished I could call my folks back home
Yeah, I decided I would drive on over
To Santa Monica & maybe
Malibu & get
Into the scenery of that
Movie with its soundtrack
By the Beach Boys

WILD RUMORS OF RAINY MCCALL
(Poem with False Dawn, Satellite Bowling Alley, All-Night Action, Plate of Yellow
Eggs, Black Dude in Gold Coat, Bottle of Bali Hi, Distant Laughter, and Mythical
City in the Clouds)

Back in Los Angeles, city of the lost angels, movie capitol of the world, Joe Harris
Wakes shuddering
Into the false dawn of neon & pale bluegreen mercury vapor pooling on the big
Empty double bed. Tiny beads of sweat gather the neon on his chest in pale bubbles
Which shimmer like raindrops, or dew in a red Appalachian sunrise. The motel
Office neon blinks its serial message through the open Venetian blinds. Joe Harris
Remembers leaving the blinds open for the night air from the ocean, or maybe it was
For the light itself, it occurs to him. & he remembers then he is not in the Holiday Inn
At the edge of Star City, West Virginia, where the interstate crossed the river. No, he
Is back in LA, following wild rumors of Rainy McCall in the city of light & projection
That could be days old, or weeks, or maybe months, not to mention years, & the room
Spins its electric promise around him like a globe

In a neighborhood where every street is a frontier, Joe Harris follows the rumors
Across a corner parking lot
A big mockup of a rocket ship sat ready for takeoff
Into the morning fog, its sprayed aluminum skin fading pink, peeling
From the relentless California light. Two huge fins climb its sides toward a revolving
Plastic sign
Saying SATELLITE BOWLING ALLEY
Pink sheen of aluminum rocket ship skin shining like a giant tuna
Landing in a cannery row, not Venus. & Gardena, California, is no Cape Kennedy
Either. Gardena
The gambling center of all of Los Angeles called Strawberry Point
In the '30s, a sleepy rich black dirt suburb with dozens of Japanese
Greenhouses
But the big money now is in the card clubs, lavish stucco
Joints under big Mexican palms, fifty, sixty tables. All night
Action
Down the night boulevards the big cars cruise like sharks under the lush
Coral-like neons, green & lavender & pink spots blooming across huge dark
Parking lots
A black dude in a gold coat, his face shining like a tropical
Orchid, opens your car door, gets you any kind of pill you can afford
To swallow. Joe Harris wanders up a set of low concrete steps shining
With that bluegreen indoor-outdoor carpet, passes
Through a big automatic glass door into the cool rush of morning
Air conditioning
SATELLITE BOWLING WELCOMES REDONDO EAGLES
Says an electronic sign over an empty circular desk

But the big lanes
Appear abandoned. So where is she? wonders Joe
Harris, in this his third day trailing around Gardena after rumors
Of Rainy McCall. & Joe Harris still doesn't have the slightest
Clue about what had happened to Rainy
McCall at the end of the last poem, that last night on the farm during that thunder
Storm to end all
Thunder storms, in the blinding rain among the old apple trees in the hillside
Orchard
The sky crackling with lightning
Most of the time Joe Harris has spent looking up people
Who don't seem to exist, not in daylight anyway
Not that it matters much. Anything beats sitting around the shabby motel
Brooding about Rainy McCall or looking
For real work. But here in the little café's submerged bluegreen aquariumlike vegetal
Light, Joe Harris kills another lost morning, eating steaming plates of yellow eggs
Waiting for his ride to Compton without expectation or even hope

The three black dudes in a fading pastel apartment
Building over in Compton seem to share
A single studio overlooking a swimming
Pool filled with decaying palm fronds. There
are a couple of gutted Cadillac convertibles in the parking
Lot & paper bags of garbage on the
Steps. Outside the door are three ancient console
Teevees, or the empty shells of
Teevees, & Joe Harris can see the blue
Morning sky reflected on their blank screens like
Some leftover travel log. It is a clear day in
LA, a rare sunny April morning, &
Joe Harris can see twenty or thirty miles
Clear across the city to the inland mountain
Ranges whose snow caps rim in the big
LA basin. The unusually clear air &
The distance itself gives the mountains
An odd, flat look, as if they are the props
In some Western Movie. The snow caps, in such
Sharp relief, look like peaks in a
Cartoon. It is as if Joe Harris could reach
Out & touch the snow. But inside
The drapes are drawn against
The light, & projection. Inside there is a lot of
Talk about mostly nothing, just some possible deals & money. The black dudes
Pass some Bali Hi, a sweet pink wine
& watch a big color teevee with the color
Tuned, or not-tuned, predominantly
To a strange sharp blue. Even
Stranger, the black dudes are not watching

A program, but instead on the blue screen
A test pattern flickers, lost
In teevee snow. The blue screen reminds
Joe Harris of something his old granddad had once
Described to him: the way a ginseng plant
Blooms. The old man told Joe Harris
He had once come upon a ginseng flowering
Deep in the mountain woods, in total
Darkness, a shimmering blue apparition
Casting its own strange light. Them
Ginsengs, the old man had said, they only
Bloom once in seven years, &
Then only at night. The old man had said
The Orientals will pay you
A pretty penny for that root. Them old
Buddhas use it to cure most everything but
Mostly they sex life. Them old Buddhas can
Get boners long after you & me & the rest of
Us real Americans is left with nothing but catfish
Bait dangling between our legs. & that ginseng
It will only grow in special soil. Radio-active
Soil, or old graveyard dirt will sometimes do the
Trick. But seeing the petals of that flower was
As rare as seeing the sweet lips of
A savior angel's pussy, the old man had said. One
Of the black dudes hands Joe Harris
The bottle of Bali Hi sweet pink wine. Bits of
Blue & pink from the soundless teevee
Drift & flick across the worn green
Carpet. The black dudes are
Shirtless & sweating mightily in
The closed, hot room, the blue light of the
Teevee making their skins appear even
Blacker, Caribbean black, Voodoo
Black. Joe Harris takes a careful pull
From the bottle of Bali Hi, a
Polynesian lady on its label smiling
Enigmatically at Joe Harris. As the wine hits
His bloodstream, Joe Harris sees with
A sudden clarity the shimmering blue apparition
Of a mountain plant blooming
In total Blackness, the sweet lips of a Savior Angel's
Pussy casting its own strange light
Over what's left of
The tragic human lifetime of Joe Harris without
The love of Rainy
McCall

The plan had seemed right. The Holiday Inn was a fancy new one, with a small
Balcony hanging over the swimming pool, & in the late evening light, Joe Harris had
Sat watching the pool lights weave up through the clear bluegreen water & ripple
Away like moonlight on a single huge tropical teardrop. There had been an afternoon
Swim, dinner, a shower, & Joe Harris had almost trusted the way the cool drink in his
Hand had said, OK, good, yes, this is real. There had been a fresh lime down in the
Ice, glowing pale blue at its edges in the light falling onto the balcony from outside
Inside, where the rumor of Rainy McCall had been drying her short black hair
Before the big bathroom mirrors, which were set up like the mirrors in a movie
Star's dressing room, where you could see your face & body from nearly any angle
& the fluorescents overhead gave your tanned flesh a deep reddish glow, catching
The pigments just right & washing your body hairs in a blonde reflection. You could
Almost imagine you really were in California after a day on white sand. Almost. I
Can't see myself, the rumor of Rainy McCall had said. Joe Harris had leaned casually
On the doorframe & tried very hard not to look at the rumor of Rainy's body. This
Had been nearly impossible. With her perfect small breasts & dark, hard nipples. The
Small waist, the curve of hip, the flat stomach that Joe Harris could almost imagine
Can't see what? Joe Harris had been real curious to know. What are you looking for
Anyhow? A tail with fur or feathers or something? The rumor of Rainy McCall had
Simply stared intently into the reflection of her own dark eyes. She had run a hand
Slowly back through her short dark hair. The rumor of Rainy always enjoyed touching
Herself. She had parted her hair & combed her jagged bangs carefully, like a flapper
Girl from a magazine ad in the '20s

No, asshole, the rumor of Rainy had said. I mean I can't see myself. I can see that
Butt, those titties, that face, the nose, the eyes, the mouth. But they are all in the way
I can't see myself down deep
The rumor of Rainy McCall joined Joe Harris on the fresh white sheets of the big
Double bed, clothes off & teevee on, bits of magenta & cyan & yellow & pink floating
Across the sheets like light in a tropical pool. A joint of good Colombian & the teevee
Light was turning to bits of snow reflecting blue, but the rumor of Rainy had not
Seemed to notice & Joe Harris had seen her begin to drift away from him, across the
Big double bed. It was exactly what he had really expected, fancy motel or not: She
Would suddenly be gone, lost in her own green eyes, the light gone from them like
The last of a Western sunset

The rumor of Rainy's dark as night hair had flared against the white pillow, her back
Curved in the blue light like a wave. Distant laughter & the faint, high-revving drone
Of a semi climbing West through the passes. But Rainy had been there, right? &
She had placed her hand on his shoulder & she had rubbed the hollow there, right?
Rainy's hand had gone stiff on his shoulder then & she had turned her face toward
The open balcony door. Tiny red-orange lights on the distant interstate had climbed
The mountain in the door like aircraft rising & blinking toward some mythical city
In the clouds. The teevee shows were off the air, & the test pattern flickered silently
Unto itself, & even the call letters were lost in snow like the last message from Earth
Bouncing off some distant satellite before flying off into outer space at the speed of
Light. The rumor of Rainy Mc Call had leaned over Joe Harris & kissed him awake
Hard & certain, & Joe Harris had awakened from a dream of the fast, dark freeway
Into the slow-motion dream of Rainy's kisses on his chest. She had bitten his nipples
Through his chest hair & chewed gently, & kissed his belly along the curve of his ribs
& then begun to kiss his penis. & then she had arched over him in near darkness, &
She had returned to his mouth, & she said: You'll never forget me, Joey. You'll never
Forget any of this. & then the rumor of Rainy had shaken out her long, dark hair in
The dream light, & somebody was crying, & there had been salt in their mouths, but
Joe Harris could no longer tell whose. Joe Harris had awakened shuddering into the
False dawn of neon & pale bluegreen mercury vapor pooling on the big empty double
Bed

It was all Joe Harris had really expected. Fancy motel or not. That she would suddenly
Be gone, vanished. Disappeared. Lost in her own green eyes, the light gone from
Them like the last of a Western sunset. Her eyes flashing a dazzling flatness & then
Gone. Joe Harris had thought about the rusting axles of the old Ford, & he wondered
About what had become of the wheels, not to mention the old Ford itself. Do you
Think I'm crazy? the rumor of Rainy McCall had asked him. No, he heard his voice
Say from some vast distance. Later, Joe Harris had decided this: That night in the
Fancy motel, Rainy had left her bodyspace, at times, for a moviespace, & moviespaces
Did not ask any questions. Moviespaces simply receive the signals, & they show the
Movies. So, Joe Harris could say that even the rumor of Rainy McCall was more a
Star than the dream of a Persian boy gone to another century or dimension near the
Ancient ruins of old Babylon

36

SECRET CEILING OF STARS
(Poem with Cheap Motel Room, Errol Flynn in His Prime, and the Ancient Egyptian
Book of the Dead)

Although Joe Harris had hitched & bused
For a week from the coast
Back East to Rainy's home state
To try to find & fetch her
Back to the farm
After a stop in Los Angeles
City of the lost angels
& the light of projection
& loss, movie capital of the world
City of salty kisses, & night air
From the Pacific Ocean tangled in the curtains of Rainy's long
Black hair
All Rainy did was complain & yell
About the crummy room
At the cheap motel
Joe Harris had rented
At the edge of Star City, West Virginia
Where the interstate crossed the river heading West
The first thing Joe Harris did when they got to the room
Was click on the tiny television set bolted
Onto the top of the dresser & find an old movie station
Which came in all snowy & full of static
Like the lightning flashes
Of tiny thunderstorms
& rolling continuously
The movie he got, though
Was one of his favorites,
An old Errol Flynn classic swashbuckler
Captain Blood or The Sea Hawk
Where Flynn was the pirate captain of a ship on the Spanish Main
Swinging boldly on ropes
In the rigging
His heroic teeth & handsome sword
Gleaming brightly
With sunlight reflected off
The Spanish Main
When he wasn't dancing about the deck
Dispensing death & mayhem
With each thrust or swipe
Of his wicked blade
In a ballet of blood
Pirouettes full of poetry & pain
Laughing playfully

Turn that Goddamn thing off
Rainy suggested
Joe Harris sat down
On the end of the lumpy bed
To sulk with dignity
Rainy didn't say another word
Joe Harris could not help but notice, however
Rainy did not bother to brush her teeth
Before flopping down
On the crummy bed
Joe Harris lay on the utter edge
Of his side of the crummy bed
Joe Harris stared at the ceiling glittering
In the television's cold polar light
Until his eyes burned
Joe Harris stared at ancient constellations
Twinkling in the Milky Way
Of that sparkly cheap motel ceiling
Constellations whose myths
Of famous heroic figures
Joe Harris knew by heart
From his brief, cherished, scientific boy days
Before some evil alien force had destroyed
His beloved, precious reflector
Telescope. East of Taurus
On the glittering ceiling
Was Orion the Hunter
The bear stars were there
Waiting to descend in the darkness
Of the giant night
For love
As a scientific boy
Joe Harris had read
That the ancient Egyptians
In accordance with their Book of the Dead
Aligned their greatest pyramids & their inner
Sepulchral chambers
With the three stars in the belt
Of Orion the Hunter in order to mirror
Heaven with their world
& to provide their beloved pharaohs
With a soft landing
In the next life
Joe Harris felt his own myth
Mirrored on the cheap motel's
Secret ceiling
That night

His own destiny
Maybe Rainy's destiny
Too, was to dwell
Among those mostly
Imagined
Stars
Joe Harris grit his heroic
Teeth. Joe Harris longed
To land softly
In some afterlife alone
Joe Harris tried not to blink
His eyes. Not even once
Joe Harris let his eyes fill with tears
Until they rolled down
The sides of his cheeks
As though a faucet had broken
In the middle
Of his face. Joe Harris was afraid
That if he closed his eyes
He might fall
Asleep
If Joe Harris fell asleep
He might roll over
Onto Rainy's side
Of the crummy bed
& their starry skins might
Touch in
The dark
Of the giant night

37

THE SECRET SCIENCE OF ANGELS AND ALIENS
(Poems with Beings Made of Dark Matter and Energy Who Move Through the
Visible World of Poetry like the Shadows of Stars)

a
Dark Energy Angel

Bright autumn sunlight flashed
Through the side windows
As we zoomed down into a big valley, where
A clear, bluegreen river angled
Toward the horizon south, &
Disappeared in the distance, the blacktop
& the shimmering
River seemed to merge
Just as they disappeared
Through the three dimensional vanishing
Point. In the side window you could see
An occasional fisherman flycasting from
The road's edge. The white filament of nylon
Line gathering the light in curves
Bright arabesques flickering
Out toward the river, in a series of
Freezeframes. You could not see the fly itself
Or any trout, but the fishermen seemed content
To cast toward some meeting point of past
& future events. You ever flyfish for
Trout? I asked Charlie Trout, who was stretched out
In the backseat, on the floor beside him
A white Styrofoam cooler filled with many
Small green bottles of icy cold Rolling Rock beer, a Yankee beer made & bottled near
Pittsburgh
Only in my worst nightmares, said Charlie Trout through his troutlike whiskers
That I am fishing in some mirrorlike pond with fast flowing waters deep in the weird
Woods of West Virginia that are thick with witches & wizards, & I land myself
From the depths of the flowing mirror
We drove on toward the vanishing point
Suddenly, at the end of a long curve
Down a mountain, I saw it: the huge, famous
Eighty-five-foot radio telescope
Set on huge stilts like the hairy legs of a giant insect. To my surprise
It did not look like my idea of
A telescope at all

It looked like a dish, a huge silvery dish
Or a shell. A giant seashell
Found on some giant beach
& in it you could hear the giant waves
Of some giant ocean flopping in from some
Giant China across the giant universe
A giant surf of giant stars

Back home in the haunted, holy
Hills & hollows of West Virginia. Charlie
Trout & I had driven down from Pittsburgh that day
In the stolen old Ford Galaxy convertible to Greenbank, West Virginia
In order to investigate this here famous
Robert C. Byrd Radio Astronomy Observatory &
Institute for Advanced Angel Studies
We were on the lookout for clues, which was our main mission that day
Charlie Trout & me
Clues to other worlds of mystery in our midst
There are a bunch of spooky
Places that serve as portals to other worlds down in our home state of West Virginia
That land of pyramidal mountains where
Silver bridges are known to drop suddenly
Into slow moving rivers
Where huge, feathered birdlike beings
With red glowing eyes & the powdery faces
Of monster moths are known to descend
Into the hills at dusk like ancient alien angels or
Fireflies from the beyond: that land where Oriental mystery
Midgets & drunken dwarves dressed all in
Black, with long, black painted fingernails
Make midnight getaways in long, black gangster
Limousines with smoky tinted windows
From the scenes of suspicious high crimes &
Misdemeanors. Due to some anomaly of nature in our home
State of West Virginia, energies
Both spiritual & natural focus &
Flow, & whip up that vortex of the inexplicable
Both holy & demonic, that tears the curtain
Between our own & other worlds
Sober up, Charlie Trout, said I. We are here
We always was here, wasn't we? said
Charlie Trout. There you go again, said I
Every time you get a dozen or so beers in you, you go & get enigmatic on me
Like you are some sort of zen hillbilly or a stoned hippie poet from San Francisco
Town

At that very moment
The old Ford's radio signal
Faded slightly, then grew sharp & clear
&, suddenly, I heard a strange, unearthly
Voice drown out the goofy gospel music
Charlie Trout had insisted on playing
On the old Ford's car radio, like the ghost
Voice of some old '40s radio cowboy singing
Star. I thought it was the ghost voice of Jimmie Rodgers or
Even old Hank hisself, at first, but I
Wasn't so sure. I wandered so aimless
Life filled with sin, went the spooky
Radio singing cowboy voice
I wouldn't let my dear Savior in
Then Jesus came like a stranger in the night
Praise the Lord I saw the light
Then, suddenly, a girl singer's sweet high hillbilly
Voice joined in the singing on the old
Radio. I thought it was the sweet dreaming
Ghost wave voice of Patsy Cline singing
At first, resurrected once again over
The radio. A sweet, forlorn, spooky voice that
Sounded like it was coming from behind
A curtain on a stage far, far
Away. But it wasn't Patsy Cline at all
The sweet, spooky voice I heard
Coming over the old
Radio was the sweet, spooky voice of Rainy McCall
I swear it
I would know that evil angel's voice
Anywhere, both inside &
Outside of my worst dreams &
Hallucinations
I saw the light, I saw the light
No more darkness, no more night
Now I'm so happy, no sorrow in sight
Praise the Lord I saw the light
Sang that sweet, spooky, evil voice in
Pure rapture over the old ribbon of radio
The song ended, & the voice
Vanished. I wheeled around to see
If Charlie Trout had also heard this thing
The sweet, spooky, evil voice of Rainy McCall singing
In rapture over the old radio
Charlie Trout, said I. Did you hear
That sweet, spooky, evil voice coming
Over the radio in pure rapture?

Charlie Trout's eyes were closed
Like he was in a trance, a half
Finished little green bottle
Of Rolling Rock beer pressed
Against his big chest
Like I always did say, that Rainy
McCall gal, she could have been a radio
Singing star as big
As the holy ghost of Patsy Cline, said
Charlie Trout, with his toothy
Gangster grin
& then it came again
That spooky, sweet, evil voice of Rainy
McCall singing, I saw the
Light, I saw the light, in pure
Harmony with that Hank
Williams ghost wave voice, Praise
The Lord I saw the light
The evil angel voice of Rainy McCall was issuing
Forth from the old Ford's radio, her
Whispery midnight black rain highway scary
Copperhead hissy lying angel voice, Rainy
McCall, that evil angel who had done
Me dirt in that old lost lifetime, that
Legendary dark heartbroke evil beauty dressed in her
Cloak of midnight & the bloody
Skins of her doomed prey, her
Feet bare & bloody from dancing
On the broken hearts & bones
Of her doomed to Hell prey, her
Black flapper girl hair all grown out again & thick
& tangled with the dark burden
Of her evil & of her lust

Some folks say that death is like stepping through a dark mirror into the real universe
Of Dark Matter
Some folks say that Dark Matter is the skeleton
The Gibson guitar of black bones for the visible world of light
Some folks say that the visible universe of light is only a wave of starry foam
On an ocean of that Dark Matter, where death & bad dreams of the world are born
But if you love the Lord of electricity & light
You can just run down that shore of shining shells of the visible beach of the visible
World of light
& do a big bellybuster into that ocean of Dark Matter
& then just swim to the next shining shore like a big fish from the Bible
With a prophet in his belly
To cough up on the beach
With a message in his mouth

Some folks say the dead forget us finally
& that the dead move away
From us finally & change their names at last
& finally we have to forget the old names of the dead, & not call out their old names
In the long giant night
No matter how much we love & miss seeing them in the visible
World of poetry
But I never forget anybody's name, & Rainy was the message
In my mouth then & forever

The Final Mystery of Rainy McCall

From behind the curtain on the stage
At the end of the auditorium, a curtain
As diaphanous as an evening in early summer
Sprinkled with the sequins of early summer stars
& flowing like a dark veil over the red mouth
Of a foreign woman singing songs of heartbreak
In another land
Voices rose up in waves
Of ritual rapture once again, in perfect
Harmony with the ghost voice of Hank Williams
I saw the light, I saw the light
& I heard the spooky, lovely voice again
Of Rainy McCall among them
A voice I would know
In my darkest sleep, the dark beauty of that sinning
Girl's breathy foreign voice
The scent of the sounds
As they echoed forth from the radio cave of her red mouth
The taste of her long, red tongue as it licked
The syllables of her song, her long, red tongue
Touching the starry midnight sky's moist constellations
Of the wet vault of her red mouth
That wide &
Generous cathedral of sweet consonants
& white teeth
Glowing like half lit bars on the back streets
Of sad, old seaports of sailor hangouts like the Barbary Shore of San Francisco
One hundred years ago
Diphthongs bent as old sailors' dicks
It was clear to me what had happened to
That Rainy McCall gal finally
The ghost of Rainy McCall had risen up
From that narrow trench on the old hillside
California farm, from under the shadows of the bent old apple
Trees, whose birdless branches of bones had
Clattered & clacked with foreign wind at night
& scary moonlight & the cries of owls over
The quiet guitar of the bones of Rainy McCall

The ghost of Rainy McCall had risen up
From that California hillside hole &
Drifted like a little cloud of rain & tears across the country
A little cloud of rain & tears like tiny dark birds, wretched
Little birds with their wings broken as their hearts & hopes, blown
By remembrance & the general, forlorn guilt
Of ghosts, & the innocence & ambiguity
Of sudden & unexpected death
Drifting with the slow, ambling indolence of death
Back to the haunted & holy hills of her home state
To revisit the ruined foreign geography of her childhood & the evil
Landscape of her daddy's hands
To haunt where she felt perfectly
Back at home with her sorrow & narrow pain, & maybe to try out
For a job as an angel singing backup in a ghost hillbilly band
An angel from
The dark side of the soul, true, but I
Knew this finally: that a dark
Angel is not necessarily
An evil angel. The voice that rose up
That day was not the voice of an evil angel
It was the voice of the ghost of a sad little hillbilly girl who
Was seeking a beautiful albeit dark song
To inhabit in death, to steal into the comforting
Soft, sad sentiments of a song, & to curl
Up there like a sleeping child, at peace & safe at last
Invisible & serene. The essence of angels
Is lightness & darkness
Equally, the motive of
Angels is to become mythic
& magical equally, like wise trolls who live under
Bridges of silver knowing the future, & forest elves, & fairies too, & leprechauns, Irish
& drunken & merry, & mystery midgets
Avatar angels all
In their special ways, magical little people
Downsized in death to make
Room for the vast unborn
I guess, who peek down from that vast
Brightness behind those pinholes some call
Constellations, searching patiently for some room
To be born. It was pleasing for me to think
That the sad spirit of Rainy McCall had
Graduated from ghost to angel at last
Knowing that the sad spirit of Rainy
McCall finally got a job as an angel singing
Backup for the ghost band of Hank
Williams was pretty to
Think about

Rainy McCall was an old sailor dick
Sucking dark angel of the Lord, true
But that was just the message in Rainy's
Mouth
& dark is not evil, is what I had come
To figure out that day. The dead forget
Us & move away & change their names finally
Finally we have to forget the old names
Of the dead, & not to call out
Their old names in the long, giant night
I had come to know this too
Charlie Trout & I had become the ghosts of our own softboiled poems
Poems of lives lived mostly outside of common expectations & experiences
The only thing either of us knew for sure was what we made up, & both of us
Fully believing that our poems were secret keys that let us in any door, &
Fully believing that true poets are people who live their poems out loud, &
Fully believing that self-discovery was finally just the process of self-invention, &
Fully believing in the need to cultivate a split personality for living life as a movie
Double or twin
& that time is just a form of foam in nature, an illusion at last
& that memory is the last duty of love
& true only to our own inconstancy
We were both avid connoisseurs & users of longing in others
& we were both well seasoned cheap ironists
Relishing ironic facts such as Steve McQueen being saved from butchery by the
Manson murderers due to
A one night stand that made him miss a dinner date with Jay Sebring & Sharon Tate
On the last bloody night of their lives
There had been a small backyard fish pond at our farm on the hill that Rainy had
Loved, & the fish in it
She had loved also, which she named after Hindu gods, both the goldfish & Koi. Why
Not just please
Explain India to me please once & for all, Rainy had begged me that last night at the
Farm
& explain how I can continue to live on three levels at the same time
Without going plumb nuts & running naked out of my own forest
Like a wild creature into the dark
Those levels being the past, the present, & the future
That last night at the farm
Rainy & I were sitting on that warm evening
At the old picnic table
By that cherished pond
Waiting for the storms
That had been rolling in over the coastal hills
From the ocean all evening
All the way from China
To hit finally

Right then though
Before the storms hit
Was a quiet, peaceful moment
For a performance of flower &
Leaf & light
Impulse to impulse, a pause in the
Geography of inner & outer turmoil
Free from the shape & tug
Of time
A landscape of silent language under glass
A Memory
Made essentially of whispers & feathers
& of leaf
A blackbird was drinking in the little falls rolling over the rocks of the cherished
Backyard pond
Feather & water
Air
Light
Feather & leaf & light
Green & glowing
Transparent
Luminous
In the light
The wet leaves shining
Like paper-thin explosions
The whole moment flashed
Like an image under
Lightning in my mind
All the past lives inside
Of the present moment
Many pasts
Nesting in a single
Now
I knew what Rainy meant by three levels of life
The rain on my skin had felt like her smoking fingertips
& then the coming storm burst upon us, clouds thick with thunder, throbbing with
Lightning like the
Throes of the birth
Of electricity, & then as though stepping through some dream gate
Rainy was gone & so began the abiding anguish of apples lost in the storm
& the fable of Rainy's final embarkment
& the prolonged celebration of her absence & the intensity of her silence

But that wasn't any throbbing of lightning
In those thunderclouds above the old apple orchard
That last night at the farm, Charlie Trout said to me, as the poem took a new direction
That wasn't no electricity being born
I was there, Peewee, Charlie Trout said to me. Don't forget
I was there & I saw what I saw
I saw those clouds filled with queer blobs of crystalline
Light like I'd seen back home in the hills at night before
When the aliens landed for love
& I saw those blue pulsating lights
Making impossible moves & turns in the giant night sky
& finally I saw that green glow out of the womb of the mothership
& I saw the poor fish leaping out from the pond
Confused & inconsolable in that green glow gulping for breath
& I saw Rainy lifting off into the sky in the green glow gulping
For breath
So it was the first moment of Rainy McCall's last fable of embarkment & departure
True
But not to death
But abduction, Charlie Trout said to me, bug-eyed with import & meaning
& right now alien pirate poets from Pluto for all we know might still yet be waiting
For Rainy's long ride to end
For Rainy's long flight to land
In the old town of Babylon
Where it is always midnight
Hour of the gypsy alien pirate poets' flight
Of abandon
When dark-haired girls
Whirl up & down & flare
& wind like flames
Across the floor
Rainy, the greatest dancer the gypsy alien poets ever saw
Spinning as in a dream
When flesh & spirit
Heat & burn by the three rivers
Blurring in the caves deep beneath the castles & cathedrals
So pick your harps & guitars & your poems
Like sweet plums from the palms
Of the gardens hanging by the three rivers
& pluck & sing the poems of Rainy dancing
In that foreign land
Sing, daughter
Of old Babylon
Doomed to destruction
Happy is the poet who repays you
According to what you have done to us

Happy is the poet who seizes your poems
By their fragile ankles
& dashes them against the rocks
By the three rivers

I heard thunder at the door
I heard its scream of yellow
& voices like foreign whispers
I heard the Oriental shadows
The moths made on the motel wall speak
In tongues to me
So feared were the shadows
Of Rainy's naked dancing body
On the walls of the motel
So feared was the shadow of her naked hunger
On the cathedral walls
Of the poem

Stop this poem, sez I to Charlie Trout. Let me get off this poem while I am alive
While I can still escape its green gravity
Before it crashes & burns
On some storied shore
Of the past
Nope, sez Charlie Trout to me
I do not know how or where this Rainy McCall poem will land
Or crash & burn
Perhaps Rainy will simply put on her gilded flapper girl golden cap
& click together the heels of her ruby slippers
& land on your doorstep calling it Kansas & yesterday

Perhaps the alien gypsy pirate poets from Pluto
For all we know
All pussy whipped & defeated
Will just dump Rainy on your doorstep
& call it even
Whereupon Rainy can simply pursue her career path as an evil dark angel
Singing backup in a ghost hillbilly band
Or maybe Rainy will give us all a break
& migrate far away to some storied beach
Become a goddess on the island
Of Hawaii say
A dark savior angel
A Pali fucky-fucky ghost goddess
Blowing sad old lonely AWOL sailor spirits
On their last shores under
The shadow of a sleeping volcano of memory & myth

You ruined Rainy for me, I remind Charlie Trout, when you fucked her in the fields of
My own farm
I never once fucked Rainy McCall
No matter how much
She begged me for it
Not for your sake
Nor for the sake of her poem
With my angel wings all electric with evil alien lust
Like I was some lowdown dark alien bean
& Rainy was my bride
For the taking

In the Star Fields of the Galaxy

The star hooker Slim runs
Silver painted nails
Back through her ink-dark punk spacecut
Tiny half moons, star clusters
Astrological animals tattooing
The star hooker Slim's hands & elegant arms
In the blur & rush of astral reruns
The big tropical albino moths cast
Exotic, Oriental shadows on the walls of the cheap
Cathedral room
Of the poem
On the tiny, silver-toned ancient transistor
Clock-radio Slim tunes
To NaWa Island folk
Magic mantra fucky-fucky singsong
The open window is rich
With trade winds from China, hot & sweet
Rich with neon, rich
With views of transmitter lights
On the volcano's rim
Slim's star hooker hands themselves
Her long, slender fingers
Are rich with rings of rubies & silver
Slim's long star hooker nails of silver
They press, they probe
The black holes & vast interstellar reaches of Joe Harris
His electric fields, his hundred billion neural gaps
The star hooker Slim's knowledge is instant
& unspoken, universal
Of where the body electric
Of Joe Harris has been hiding
The star hooker Slim whispers
Visions of his body's electric future
In the star fields of the galaxy
Slim's long, star hooker, savior angel silver
Nails scratch softly
Down deep, deep into the ancient itch
The secret yin-shoal urge
The sacred memory currents
The body oceanic
Of Joe Harris
Scratch, touch, touch in the meridians
Of transformation & memory
Of Rainy McCall

Scratch across the galactic
Shelf & back again, layer
On shifting layer of past
Pleasure & pain, the acupuncture
Planets called past pleasure, past pain
Of Rainy McCall
Her hands, her long fingers of silver orbits
Her silver nails deep
In his dharma-tao, his electric nakedness
The light of his neon
Like light through coral, light through shell
Hey, sailor, sez the star hooker Slim
To Joe Harris
You want to dance, man?
Not with this bloody butt, I don't
Sez Joe Harris

d

A High Midnight Movie Mass of Execution

We took another room for the next night at the poem, nothing fancy, not crummy
Either
With a new model teevee & working remote
I watched Rainy McCall step from under the shadow of her own star
Into a soaring stone winter cathedral with the pride & grace
Of tragic, Renaissance royalty
A queen on her way to the chopping block
For the high crime of her dark beauty & ancient religious bloodline
Mary, Queen of Scotland
The soaring stone cathedral flickered with the flames of Christmas candles
Like the shadows of summer flowers or small black birds on the stone walls
Of the poem & in the high midnight mass of Rainy's black hair
Like a snow of stars
I watched Rainy stride through the stone poem
Katharine Hepburn in all her tragic black & white beauty, mystery, & grace
On flickering late night television
I watched Rainy bend her slim, elegant neck fearlessly for the blow
I saw the splashed blood
Of severed summer flowers & a sacrificial solstice movie queen at the moment of her
Death
Splattered over the stones of the floor & soaring walls of Rainy's poem
So feared was the shape of Rainy's animal eloquence & the dancing
Shadow of her flame
So feared was Rainy's midnight mystery & grace, which were the shadows
Of a burning star
So feared were the flames
That climbed Rainy's legs
So feared were the shadows of Rainy & my hunger as they danced on
The walls of the poem
There in the ruined winter cathedral
Of her poem
But the midnight stars burned behind
The blue, blue windows of
That giant motel of midnight movies
&
Imagination
Everything dies, daughter, now that's a fact
But everything that dies maybe someday comes back
Through those huge open blue windows
Behind the stars
Yes, we took that room at the poem
For another giant night, daughter,
Where in the elegance, mystery, grace, &
Beauty of black & snowy white movies we danced until dawn

112

Existence is chance
So dance, daughter
Dance
Even when you leave
Bloody footprints
In the snow

The Old Sorcerer's Daughter

I have been for a long time
In the motel of this poem
Where Rainy once was
Where Rainy once rested
Where Rainy no longer returns
No words written in lipstick red
As blood
On the bathroom mirror where
Rainy once did makeup
I hear the echo of keys rattling in other doors down the long hallway
I sit on the bed watching the silent television set
I kick off the bloody blue suede shoes I wore to
Dance. Now I lay me back on the crummy bed
In twisted sheets that smell like surf
Here are only the two of us, I say to my secret self
Only my imagination & the poem in this crummy motel room.
But if I think hard, Rainy was here too
A beautiful, black-haired Flapper Princess who
Glided on my slick, glowing skin
Who danced wetly on my knees
Making the exotic Oriental shadows of tropical moths
On the walls of our cathedral poem
Here where Rainy once mirrored
& where Rainy no longer returns to mirror
Now outside the door
With no key to be found
The low skies thick & dark with clouds
Of storms rolling down from the volcanoes
Like currents of lava
On the road there is no traffic, no people
I confess, this does not happen so often
To leave a poem alone
Lost in my own solitude
& loneliness
Now outside the door
With no key to be found
Somebody has already put away the day
The morning is like the bitter embrace
Of a bitter sinister foreigner
In a climate of absence & oblivion
I turn around quickly to look over my shoulder

The road behind is like a dry river bed
Lined by cold campsites abandoned for generations
By those ancient blue warrior
Tribes, who landed on these islands in long canoes, covered with battle story tattoos
Fierce & unforgiving
& then peopled the forests around the rims
Of the sleeping volcanoes, where they beat drums, chanted, & tossed
Their green-eyed virgin daughters into the fiery mouth
Of Pali before gods with faces of stone
I leave bloody footprints behind me
On the cracked pavement
I will be easy prey to follow
The neon sign in the window
Of the motel office blinks VACANCY
With uncanny persuasion
The bowling alley next door
Is locked down tight, closed to customers
I stop to look in a window
Just in case
Where there is a dim inner glow like
A refrigerator opened secretly in
The middle of the night. Or the frail light
At the end of a long, dark hallway
Brown shards of broken beer bottle glass
Cover an empty playground
On the corner a caution light blinks
As precisely as a beating heart
A fine rain like mist or tiny tears
Dampens my face as I follow
The broken lines
Of the poem back toward
The title
Where it all began
In the first place
I search my pockets again
For the lost key
Turn them inside out
At the hut of the old sorcerer
Near the shore
I stop to ask
For another key
I sit down on a stone bench
Beside the old sorcerer
In his garden of ancient orchids & pet
Lizards
At the edge of ocean
I see now he is nothing but an old naked
Blue warrior with a tiny sword

He calls a key
Which he hands to me gladly with the toothsome grin
Or grimace
Of a skull
In a window opposite where we sit
& chant under our breaths
Like the quiet graveside whispering at a burial
Behind a torn curtain translucent
As an old sail or map of skin
I see the old sorcerer's own naked blue daughter
She has the black hair & green eyes
Of a sacrificial virgin
Dangerous tattoos that tell the story
Of her love life cover her pale, elegant arms, delicate shoulders, &
Blue breasts
Which she likes to pretend
Are invisible
I see my reflection
In her green eyes
Where my face glows
Like a dead man
Awake for his own funeral
I smile at her, apologetic & sad
But she simply shivers & laughs at me
As she
Touches herself
I put the key in my pocket
& walk away West
Through the moldering ruins of the city
In the long shadow
Of the smoking volcano
The poem has grown late
Only
The old motel remains open
& ready for business
Shining like a mirror
In the moonlight

I remove the remote
From my pocket
Desiring only
To make amends now
& click it to
Another poem
Which begins with a long canoe sailing
At sunset
Without us
Toward the West
The last long canoe home
It is said
For a generation
Sailing back to home
Where a thousand years ago ancient surf
Sorcerers dipped fingers into the sea, feeling
The shape of waves to prophesize the safety of distant landfall
Dots of volcanic islands a thousand miles away
Floating upon a vast uncharted sea
Like a lei of tropical flowers
Which launched a generation of blue warriors
& green-eyed virgins
The old sorcerer's daughter & I return
To the open motel
To see if anything
Is on
We have not already seen
Or imagined
I can smell her tropical naked perfume
Across the night
In the dark
The love stories of
Her blue tattoos glow
On her luminous skin
Like thin neon tubing
& blue fingerprints
Blink like tiny maps
I can hear rain falling like cinders on the roof
I can hear smoke rubbing its back
On the window panes
& the purring of the past
A phone is ringing in another room
Like a call from tomorrow
& voices coming from an old radio program from the past
& the gentle sighs of neon signs in the night
Snowflakes falling from
The television onto the floor
Of the new poem

& a siren from somewhere
In the smoking ruins of the city
Or the scream of a green-eyed virgin
From high on the volcano
There are the juicy sounds of sex from another room
Followed by the sounds of sobbing
Rainy touches herself
In the starless dark, blind
With utter
Inwardness
Smoldering & sorrowful
For both the great & the mostly
Forgotten loves of her life
Now I lay me down
To sleep, I say
Then I say, So
Be it, Amen, marveling that the new poem's night is still
A place of mystery & grace
Full of voices from a faraway future only
Faintly remembered
The soft, mostly forgotten songs
Of vanished green-eyed mermaids

THAT'S ALL SHE WROTE, FOLKS.

63978187R00074

Made in the USA
Charleston, SC
18 November 2016